We will send you a free catalog on request. Any titles not in your local bookstore can be purchased by mail. Send the price of the book plus 50¢ shipping charge to Leisure Books, P.O. Box 511, Murray Hill Station, New York, N.Y. 10156-0511.

Titles currently in print are available for industrial and sales promotion at reduced rates. Address inquiries to Nordon Publications, Inc., Two Park Avenue, New York, N.Y. 10016. Attention: Premium Sales Department.

A WOMAN CALLED

Golda

NOVELIZATION BY
MICHAEL AVALLONE
BASED ON
THE TELEVISION FILM
"A WOMAN CALLED GOLDA"
WRITTEN BY
HAROLD GAST AND STEVEN GETHERS

LEISURE BOOKS  NEW YORK CITY

A LEISURE BOOK

Published by

Nordon Publications, Inc.
Two Park Avenue
New York, N.Y. 10016

INGRID BERGMAN      NED BEATTY
FRANKLIN COVER      JUDY DAVIS
ANNE JACKSON      ROBERT LOGGIA
LEONARD NIMOY   JACK THOMPSON

# A WOMAN CALLED GOLDA

MUSIC BY MICHEL LEGRAND
ASSOCIATE PRODUCER
   MARILYN HALL
EXECUTIVE PRODUCER
   HARVE BENNETT
WRITTEN BY HAROLD GAST
   AND STEVEN GETHERS
PRODUCER GENE CORMAN
DIRECTED BY ALAN GIBSON

# INTRODUCTION

### by Marilyn Hall
### Associate Producer of *A Woman Called Golda*

Television shows don't just happen, they are planned and discussed months in advance. Thus the spring of 1981 found me in London, talking with Ingrid Bergman about the possibility of her portraying Golda Meir in a television mini-series about the life of that great lady. One of the visionaries and dreamers who coaxed the State of Israel into being, nursed it through its difficult formative period and later became its Prime Minister, Golda seemed to be the stuff of which movie heroines are made.

Miss Bergman acknowledged that portraying the "Mother of Israel" would be an interesting challenge. However, she could foresee problems in the fact that there was no physical resemblance between herself and Mrs. Meir. "How can a tall Swede with an angular frame portray a woman who is short and has a rather ample figure?" she asked. With her slight Swedish accent in evidence, she added, "I don't even speak Jiddish!"

But in spite of her doubts, the deal was arranged. That's how it happened that, on this hot Friday afternoon in August, I met Ingrid Bergman's plane as it touched down at the airport in Israel. The airport was almost deserted, with the mesmerizing calm that descends on the whole country from before sundown on Friday till the end of the Sabbath observance, twenty-four hours later. Miss Bergman's plane was the last one that would arrive before the Sabbath shutdown.

7

Though not a publicity seeker, Ingrid Bergman is conditioned to having newsmen and photographers around documenting her comings and goings. She seemed rather startled to see the scant handful of people assembled to greet her, and I hastened to reassure her of her welcome. We had purposely planned her arrival at this time, I explained, in order to keep a low profile and protect her from unnecessary intrusions by the media.

"How refreshing," Miss Bergman commented, smiling.

True professional that she is, Ingrid Bergman was soon absorbed in planning the research she wanted to do before filming began. Archives, films, cassettes—anything that pictured Mrs. Meir or documented her history—had to be studied. Miss Bergman was particularly anxious to hear recordings of Golda's lusty laugh. In the next few days we journeyed to the Israeli TV station in Jerusalem to see documentaries; to the Rad Archives on Mt. Scopus; then back to United Studios north of Tel Aviv to replay a show on which Golda Meir was featured. An Israeli version of "This Is Your Life," the show pictured not only Golda herself, but practically every living person who had been important to her in one way or another.

Miss Bergman studied Golda's gestures, her hand patterns, the way she carried her purse, her ramrod authoritative walk, her endless smoking. Gradually the transformation began; Miss Bergman's mannerisms, gestures, even her voice quality, became those of Mrs. Meir. Government employees and others who had worked with Golda or known her personally rushed to the location site to see for themselves, and were greatly impressed.

As one remarked, "For a moment I thought Golda was in the next room, that she had returned, that she still lives."

The fact that the people who knew her called her "Golda"—she was that kind of person—added to the difficulties involved in trying to film Mrs. Meir's life. Since she was both a "founding mother" and heroine of Israel, and a very vital, deeply loved woman, the movie had to show her human side while still doing justice to the momentous events that made her world famous. Yet the

8

records usually fail to tell anything about the personal doubts and fears, and inner struggles, of such almost larger-than-life people. It is left to the creative instincts of the writer to depict, with subtle shading, the human being behind the news stories.

Another problem was that there was so much richness in Golda Meir's life, so much material that could not be captured in a four-hour film, that many highly dramatic events had to be omitted. One such omission was the whole record of Golda's life as Israel's first envoy to Russia. It was the ultimate irony: On September 3, 1948, three months after the declaration of the State for which she had labored, at the moment of its birth, Golda had been sent out of the country. We could not depict life in the Hotel Metropole, where for the first time the Israeli flag fluttered in the chill Moscow air.

As word spread of Golda's presence in the city, a groundswell of Zionist sympathy took hold of the "underground" Jewish community. Putting fear of reprisal behind them, forty thousand Jews appeared at the Moscow synagogue, and Golda—a symbol of freedom in the subjugated crowd—was engulfed by them. So moved was she by this demonstration that she tearfully thanked them for "remaining Jews." Five months later the Soviet government retaliated with the first of many repressive measures the Jews were to suffer in the years to come— including the closing down of newspapers and printing presses, and the banning of the Yiddish theater.

Along with such major deletions, in the interests of clarity much inconsequential data was weeded out: minor political positions Golda held at one time or another, unimportant diplomatic missions she undertook, friendships and family relationships that did not affect the mainstream of her life, and so forth. Then it was necessary to make some compromises between facts and storytelling; for instance, *Ephraim Ben Ariel* is a fictional character, actually a composite of several people who were influential in molding Golda's career or her personal life. Innocent inaccuracies might also have been committed; for instance, with her traditional background it's possible that Golda would never have bought meat from an Arab shopkeeper, as one scene in the movie shows her doing. But then again, under the stress of poverty perhaps she did buy where it was cheapest; poverty can make one do desperate things.

The writer also chose to change the date of Golda's sentimental journey to the 4th Street School in Milwaukee. The date of the actual visit was 1969, but in the film was changed to 1977. For dramatic purposes, it was felt Golda should be summoned to Jerusalem from Milwaukee to meet Sadat.

Along with these specific problems, every production has its disasters which at the time seem earthshaking but afterward are remembered laughingly. This production had its share. The wind machine gobbled up the Egyptian flag as it was being lowered, thereby putting both out of commission. Miss Bergman's double got wedged in the Piper Cub and had to be extricated with much finesse from the joy stick. A Chassidic (ultra-religious) group stood in front of our camera to prevent us from working on a religious holiday. But the biggest disaster that day was the discovery that cast, crew, cameras, props and everything else had to be moved away from one location site—we had unwittingly set up shop in front of the house of the Chief Rabbi of Tel Aviv.

As we re-created history we were living through history in the making. We met Moshe Dayan, who received us at Zahala and gave us a tour of his gracious home and artifact-laden garden. He walked tentatively, a frail figure, his one eye weakened by recent surgery. But his voice became stronger as he spoke of Jewish culture and archeology, so it was possible to glimpse in him the charismatic, fiery orator of old. Miss Bergman was enthralled by this warrior, this legendary hero. She posed with him for pictures; these are among his last published photographs. And as she did with everyone who knew Golda Meir, she questioned him at length about the late Prime Minister.

The most poignant memory for everyone involved in the movie was the night following Sadat's assassination. We were filming the celebration of the founding of the State of Israel in 1948. The location was Bialik Square, the first municipality building in Tel Aviv, in a neighborhood built by the Jewish pioneers. For our purposes the site had been transformed into Independence Square, and it was our second night of working there. By nine o'clock there had still been no final confirmation of Sadat's death. Rumors were rife, spreading like brushfire, dominating the conversation between takes, casting a Kafkaesque quality on the young people dancing the *hora,* clapping and singing.

Miss Bergman was stunned by the news. "Impossible!" she said. "Why don't people appreciate life? The whole world is going crazy; look what happened to the Pope!"

The situation was a painful contrast to the preceding day's shooting, when the boisterous enthusiasm of the young *kibbutzniks* and Russian immigrants cast as extras continued after the cameras had stopped rolling. Tonight people gathered in knots listening to transistors, or huddled around an automobile whose radio carried the communiques. The young people speculated on their future: Would they be called up, would the peace process crumble? Some wondered about their friends who were spending the last vacation days before school started scuba diving in the Red Sea. Were they in danger? Still others were cynical: "It's a trick, saying he's dead, so they can catch the assassins." (Games of intrigue are part of Middle Eastern thinking.)

"He had people around him who believed as he did," said an army reservist.

"We'll never give back the Sinai," said another.

Overhead we heard the F-15's. Yes, Israel was on the alert, but not, I found out later, because of the assassination. A few days earlier an Israeli mission boat had run aground in Saudi Arabia and the Saudis had not been cooperative about its return. (After some very strong warnings the boat was eventually released.) Now, the radio crackled with static as the BBC confirmed Sadat's death. *Met! Met? Met!* The word was relayed through the crowd. Dead. Some of the older people cried as the finality seeped in. When the young people were called for the next take, somehow the clapping and singing lacked electricity and energy. The next day the Israeli flag was at half mast, and for a week the country's mood was somber. But then the Israelis picked up the mechanics of living, wary still, yet confident that peace would continue.

The filming of Golda Meir's story required over ninety actors, American, English and Israeli; two thousand extras; over a hundred crew members; fifteen hundred costumes; scores of antique vehicles and obsolete war machinery; countless wigs, moustaches, props and artifacts of all kinds. Before the production was finished the commissary had served over ten thousand meals to the cast and crew. But finally all the pieces came together and the life of Golda Meir was captured on film.

In the final shot for the movie, Miss Bergman was on her fifth take, a rather unusual situation for an actress who usually wraps up a scene in one or two. Finally she looked at the director and said, "I don't think I can get it right." After a moment's pause she added, "I think I don't want the movie to end. I've gotten to know Golda and I'm going to miss her."

I hope you, the reader, will also grow to know and love Golda Meir through reading her story. As Golda once said, "Zionism and pessimism are not campatible."

# BOOK ONE

*Palestine*

*"If I am not for myself, who will be for me?
But if I am for myself only, what am I?"*

—Hillel, Hebrew sage

## Genesis

In the Milwaukee of 1977, motorcades and lavish automotive processions were not all that common. Yet on this particular day, at this special time, the several dark limousines, preceded and flanked by cruising motorcycles bearing smartly uniformed policemen, seemed to journey through the modern city streets unnoticed. There were no streams of newspaper confetti from the windows of the buildings bordering the thruways and thoroughfares, no wildly shouting crowds lining the sidewalks. Indeed, this motorcade had more the air and solemnity of a funeral procession.

Inexplicably, but with that touch of ironic good humor that tinged all of her inmost thoughts, Lou Kaddar wondered why. Seated in the guest-of-honor limousine, beside the woman to be acclaimed this day, Lou Kaddar's thoughts were remarkably definite and decisive. A handsome woman of sixty, with firmly chiseled features, the lady who had been secretary, confidante and friend to one of the most renowned females of the twentieth century was hard put to marshal her thoughts and opinions in formal order. Was it ever so easy to describe Golda Meir?

*"How should I describe her? To people all over the world she was one of the great women of this century. Some say she was the very greatest. It is hard for me to judge. To me she was my long-time dear friend. . . ."*

The motorcade had slowed, the motorcycles were braking to a stop, the line of limousines was bearing into the curb. They stopped before an ancient structure, low and wide, whose cement facade showed its age. Its row upon row of windows bore evidence that this was a place of children and fun, and knowledge, and growing up—a school building. But there were no children about, the place seemed deserted at the moment.

Lou Kaddar gazed affectionately at the elderly woman seated next to her: at the stoic face with its tiny bun of gray hair rising above the features which had weathered and lived through so much; at the boxy dress, the prim matching pocketbook, the ramrod-straight posture, the hands folded prayerfully across the lap. Lou Kaddar smiled at the woman she loved above all others.

*"I remember, when I first went to work as her assistant, I called her 'Mrs. Meyerson'—that was her name before it was changed to Meir. On the second day she said to me, 'Would it hurt you to call me Golda, like everyone else does?'"*

People suddenly stood before the school building now. There was the principal, Mr. Macy, who had arranged all this, smiling and very nervous. Beside him was a tall, plump black woman, beaming with pleasure. Several of the uniformed policemen surrounding them, with their holstered guns visible, were nodding, pointing, indicating their awareness that a great day was about to dawn—a great moment.

Golda Meir, still vital, still formidable though in her late seventies, was puffing on a small cigarette almost like a beginner.

"Golda," Lou Kaddar said softly. "Your cigarette."

"What's the matter, you're afraid I'll die young?"

The famous voice was soft too but tinged with good humor—unfailing good humor, the gallows wit so much a part of Jewish life.

"The children," Lou Kaddar said. "We're almost there."

Golda Meir's keen gray eyes understood.

"Oh. Yes."

She snuffed out the cigarette in the ashtray at her elbow. There was no more to be said. The vehicles were pulling up and doors opening, disgorging occupants. Mr. Macy was hurrying forward, hand extended in warm welcome. Pouring from the massed limousines, tall, dressed-alike, grim-faced security men scanned the surrounding buildings and every available inch which could harbor trouble or troublemakers. Lou Kaddar handed Golda Meir from the interior of the special limousine to the sidewalk. Mr. Macy babbled greetings and the black woman smiled even wider. The policemen fanned out in a cordon of protection.

Golda Meir smiled the smile that seventy years of travail and torment and hope and survival had taught her.

From within the ancient cement walls of the school building came a rising chorus of youthful voices, welcoming their distinguished visitor— the woman they had heard so much about yet knew so little, the very famous woman called Golda Meir.

"*Kol od balevov p'ni moh*

*Nefesh yehudi homiyoh. . . .*"

Golda Meir smiled as she entered the building, with Lou Kaddar at her elbow as she had been for a long, long time now.

It was like being home again, hearing the songs at sunset.

Like being in Israel.

*God bless the children!*

The black woman, who proved to be the assistant principal, hurried up the steps in her wake, shaking her head and marveling at the wonder of it all. Mr. Macy was in seventh heaven, a principal's paradise. Think of it—Golda Meir at his school!

Fourth Street School was on the map now, forever and a day.

Behind them all, the security men and the uniformed policemen kept their eyes alert, their hands close to their guns. Nothing must happen to Mrs. Golda Meir, the ex-Prime Minister of Israel—not in their town, at any rate.

The singing voices increased in volume as the guest of honor was led toward the school auditorium, moving slowly but with a firm tread.

Lou Kaddar smiled proudly. The Hebrew words were like a warm blanket of welcome, bridging the gulfs, the chasms, the differences of all time and place and politics. They were the sound of freedom unabated.

*"Ul fa'ate misroch kodimoh*

*Ayin le'tzion zofiyoh. . . ."*

Golda Meir paused in wonder at the very threshold of the school auditorium. The singing voices had risen in volume, filling the walls with melody. Her surprise was total, complete. The voices, unified and beautiful, were issuing from a a sea of shining black faces—little people of the world, all dressed up for this occasion, booming the sacred words and phrases of a far-off land they had never known or could know. The adults flanking Golda Meir—Mr. Macy, the assistant principal and Lou Kaddar—all halted as she turned in speechless amazement. The shrewd eyes had misted over, the stoic expression had crumpled into awe. *Can you believe this?* was the unspoken thought of Golda Meir as she shook her head incredulously and fought for equanimity.

*". . .Od lo ovdoh tikvotenu*
*Hatikvoh shnos eil payim. . . ."*

19

The black children sang away, gathering strength and enthusiasm as they mastered the difficult words. Now the staff of Fourth Street School was joining in—the teachers, some black, some white. Surrounding them and adorning the walls of the auditorium were a flock of decorative banners and posters, proclaiming SHALOM and WELCOME, GOLDA MEIR.

"... *Lihyos am chafsi b'artzeinu*
*Eretz tzion vi Yerushalayim. . . .*"

Tears filled Golda Meir's eyes. Her heart soared. Her body trembled with a happiness beyond belief.

The singers repeated the last chorus of the song: "*Lihyos am chafsi b'artzeinu eretz tzion vi Yerushalayim. . . .*"

The singing ended and a vast hush filled the auditorium. The children waited, eager, expectant, poised for important things, for fulfillment of all they had planned.

A little girl, prettily and starchily dressed, came forward shyly, her eyes big and round. A small bouquet of flowers was clutched in her tiny hand like an explosion of colors. "*Shalom, Golda,*" the young voice bravely whispered, extending the flowers to the tall old lady before her.

Golda Meir took the flowers gently, overcome. The auditorium was a wavering haze before her tear-filled vision. Impulsively she knelt, hugging the child to her bosom. At that gesture the

20

auditorium shivered and thundered with applause. Waves of approbation echoed down from the four walls. It was a great moment.

The deafening applause continued as Mr. Macy helped Golda Meir to her feet and led her to the platform, with the assistant principal and Lou Kaddar beaming in their wake. The clapping and demonstration of warmth and welcome settled down. Golda Meir clasped her hands prayerfully in her lap once more, her fingers entwined about the bouquet of flowers. Mr. Macy stepped to the lectern. His joy could not be contained as he opened the proceedings in a brisk, authoritative voice.

"With the singing of *Hatikvoh*, the national anthem of Israel, we welcome to the Fourth Street School its most distinguished graduate, Mrs. Golda Meir, former Prime Minister of Israel."

Again the applause, briefer this time but no less enthusiastic and welcoming. All eyes in the auditorium were riveted upon the tall, ramrod-straight woman in the boxy dress, with the tiny bun of hair, as she took the place at the lectern vacated by Mr. Macy. The aloneness of her figure up there, the unadorned simplicity of her, had a powerful effect. The audience hushed, waiting.

Golda Meir gazed out lovingly at the sea of shining black faces.

Her voice, low but firm, reached out from the platform—a voice one would not have believed had ever been raised in anger.

"*Shalom* . . . *shalom* to you. It's a beautiful word. It means 'hello,' and 'goodby.' But what it really means is *peace*—may peace be with you."

She paused, fighting the tide of emotion which had swept over her, suddenly and unbidden, by this return to her old school and by all these beautiful young black children singing the songs of her homeland.

"Mr. Macy, members of the faculty, distinguished guests, and children—very dear children—I tried to think of how to express my feelings on being with you in my old school where, as I look around, it's amazing! Nothing seems to have changed except me."

Veteran speaker that she was, she waited for the laughter that followed. Then she continued, "What comes to my mind is an old saying of the ancient Jewish sage Hillel, who lived around the time of Christ. Hillel said, 'If I am not for myself, who will be for me? But if I am for myself only, what am I?'"

She paused again, briefly, her eyes mesmerizing the audience. "And 'If not now, when?' These words have meant a great deal to me, all my life. I will tell you why. . . ."

There was so much to tell, all on one golden morning, in a mere few hours. Her life as a little girl in Kiev, Russia, in those terrible days of 1902. As a teenager with her family. As a young uncertain bride with Morris Myerson, the sign painter. She could tell of living in a *kibbutz*, that commune of the poor; of becoming a young mother in a terrible land; of being labor minister in the Israeli goverment, then foreign minister at the United Nations; of being Prime Minister of

Israel and meeting President Nixon and Secretary of State Kissinger. All that and much more, so much more. . . .

Lou Kaddar had lived through a lot of it with her—Lou, who forever worried and fretted about her and her way with the important or even the unimportant people of the world.

Even now, as all the children and the adults listened with rapt attention in that auditorium of the Fourth Street School, wise old Lou Kaddar was fearful for her outspoken friend Golda Meir, who only knew how to speak the truth and never turned from it.

There was only one Golda Meir.

*"At the end of her speech, Golda invited questions from the children. This worried me, because she had very little patience with questions. . . ."*

Lou Kaddar glanced out anxiously at the crowd as Golda asked for questions. She could not help being worried. *"I remember a diplomatic reception when I was translating into French for her. I said, 'The Minister asks how you arrived here.' She stared at me. 'You don't know we came by airplane?'*

*"I said, 'Yes, madame, but I merely translate. You are the one who must answer.' She said: 'Tell him we came by donkey.'"*

*"But for the questions of children,"* Lou Kaddar mused, *"she had infinite patience."*

A black girl, bright and cute had stood up. "I want to ask you, Mrs. Meir, were you a good student? Did you get good marks?"

Golda Meir reflected on that, smiling. "Well, I remember a few A's, some B-plusses, some B's. Below that, for some reason my memory doesn't work."

The children whooped with laughter. Mr. Macy stepped up to Golda's side.

"Mrs. Meir's memory is too modest. We looked up her record. She was Valedictorian of her class."

Golda said, "I hope they didn't also notice that my teachers commented I was too talkative."

There was great laughter from the children at that. Mr. Macy singled out another raised hand. "Next question."

This time a boy rose to his feet, his dark face curious. "Mrs. Meir, how come you left?"

For a moment, Golda was startled. "Left what?"

"America," the boy said. "Why did you leave America to go to Israel?"

Golda Meir grew calmer and a great comprehension glowed on her face. Smiling tenderly, she looked down at the little boy from her great height on the platform—the little boy and all his schoolmates.

"Oh, that's a fine question. Believe me, if I had been born in America, I might never have left. But my earliest experiences were very different from an American child's." Her voice rose in a statement no less poignant for its simplicity and brevity. "I was born in Russia. . . ."

And from that moment forward she held her audience of black and white, children and adults,

24

in the palm of her weathered hand. For a timeless hour the Fourth Street School did not exist. The story of Gold Meir unfolded—a horror story, a love story, a war story, a Life Story.

It was the stuff that great people and great events are made of, a story no one had ever heard before. And might never hear again.

It was one woman's story—and what a story! How could anyone have lived such a life, even in that day and age?

## *Over There*

---

They were a small mob of people, all of them
males and most of them drunk, not only with the
contents of the wine bottles they had drained but
with the fear of something they did not understand and only partially believed. But, believing
or not, fear had all of them in its grip. And now, as
they lurched and shouted and swayed down the
middle of the road in the town of Kiev, Russia, the
monstrous evil had been formed. It was the year
1902 and Russia was in the very birththroes of its
persecution of all those who practiced the Hebrew faith and wore the Star of David. It was
nighttime, of course, for Evil is always practiced
by night, under cover of darkness.

The mob held aloft flaming torches or bran-
dished stout sticks and old cavalry sabers. Their
drink-slurred voices roared out hoarse threats
and obscenities as they progressed along the
rutted roadway, scanning the fronts of the squat
little houses they passed. Overhead a faint moon
gleamed dully in the night sky.

Within the home of Moshe Mabovitch the sound of hammer blows echoed loudly. No one had to ask what Moshe Mabovitch was doing as he nailed wooden planks across his front door with determined zeal. His adoring wife Bluma stood at his side, where she had always been, ready with yet another plank. Neither of them felt the need to discuss the wisdom of this joint effort. Both had seen this coming for days—this terror, this persecution that was beyond all common sense and belief.

Huddled in one corner of the family living room were their two daughters, Sheyna, age fifteen, and Golda, a bewildered and curious five-year-old. As their father hammered away purposefully, Golda tugged at her older sister's dress.

"Why is Papa doing that?"

"There's a *pogrom*," Sheyna responded, frightened.

"What's a *pogrom*?"

"Sssh. Be quiet. Don't talk so much."

"But what is it?" Golda persisted, as little children will when a mystery is not explained at all.

"Golda, I said quiet!" Sheyna snapped despairingly, her eyes fixed on the backs of their beloved father and mother.

Beyond the walls of the house, in the darkened roadway, rioting men paused to swig at their bottles. The terrible shouting continued. Moshe Mabovitch nailed the last plank in place and brushed off his work-worn hands. The hooting and howling of the mob seemed to come through the very walls. His wife Bluma took one of his hands in her own. Her dark eyes mirrored the tragedy and insanity of it all.

Golda shook her blonde head. "What are they yelling out there, Sheyna?"

"I don't know," Sheyna lied. "I can't hear."

"I can," Golda crowed. "Something about the Jews. Don't you hear it?"

"Yes," her sister said.

"We killed somebody!" Golda exclaimed in childish awe. "The Jews killed somebody!"

"Goldie," Sheyna begged. "Will you stop talking?"

"Who did we kill, Sheyna?" Children always require answers.

"Their Lord," Sheyna answered flatly. "They say we killed their Lord."

Golda frowned, her child's face puckered with incomprehension. "I didn't kill anybody."

The roaring of the mob outside was suddenly louder, closer, terrifyingly near. Moshe Mabovitch turned, eyes wide, lips working against spellbinding inner terror. "*Put the lamps out!*" His voice was wailing, fearful. The beast outside was coming to devour his family.

Quickly, Bluma and Sheyna moved to obey him. They extinguished the two kerosene lamps which illuminated the Mabovitch living room; then they cowered, waiting, listening in the dark. Outside, sabers clicked and rattled. Then an empty bottle came crashing through the window, splintering glass and sending fragments to the black floor. Bluma Mabovitch hugged her chil-

29

dren to her bosom and closed her eyes. Moshe Mabovitch stiffened, hands knotted into fists. His eyes were wary, waiting for the critical moment, the time of trial. And then amazingly, abruptly, the roar of the crowd diminished. The shouts trailed off into the troubled night.

"I think, please God," Moshe Mabovitch muttered, "they're going away."

Sheyna Mabovitch trembled in the darkness. "What if they come back, Papa?"

Helplessly, her father held up his hands. "We just have to keep the lamps out and be very quiet."

"Is that all we're going to do, Papa?"

"What else *can* we do?" Moshe Mabovitch's anguish was limned in the five words. He turned from his daughter in a mixture of self-contempt and total mistrust of his fellow man.

There was a long moment of silence in the darkness, a time in which heartbeats could be measured.

And then Golda's young voice said once more, "What's a *pogrom*?"

Sheyna, lips trembling, slender body shuddering, stared at her little sister in the gloom. She wanted to answer, wanted to tell the child, but what came from her mouth was a reaction of anger and fear. "Do you have to keep talking all the time?"

No one answered her, least of all little Golda.

The Mabovitches, father, mother and two daughters, trembled in the frightening darkness.

When the last sounds of the violent mob had been swallowed up by the night, Sheyna flung herself face down across the bed in one corner of the living room. She was deeply upset and fighting for control, but it would not come. She sobbed fiercely. Her mother and father stood with their arms about each other, sharing a moment of comfort. Little Golda went to her big sister and knelt to put her soft face close to Sheyna's.

"I'm sorry, Sheyna," she whispered.

Sheyna shook her head without looking at her.

"I'm not angry at you, I'm angry at Papa. Because there *is* something better to do than hide in the dark and he doesn't want me to do it." Suddenly she lifted herself, bursting with purpose and decision. "Well, I'm going to do it anyway, even if I could be sent to Siberia."

"Why?" Golda said, perplexed.

"For being a Zionist," Sheyna explained in a low voice. "There's a group that I know about and I'm going to join. I'm going to be a Zionist."

"What's that, Sheyna?"

"It's . . . well, it's Jews from all over the world getting together to make . . . a country of their own. *Our* own—in Palestine. So we can live like other people." Sheyna's expression was proud. "Nobody will dare hurt us and kill us just because they want to."

"Where's Palestine?"

"You know!" Sheyna took her little sister by the shoulders. "It's the Promised Land that God gave the Jews—where we used to live, where King Solomon built the Temple!"

Golda's eyes grew round with expectation and

wonder. "Can we go there now?"

"No. But someday, we hope." Sheyna Mabovitch sighed.

"You know something," Golda Mabovitch said, firmly. "Just as soon as I can go there, I'm going."

From across the darkened room, Moshe Mabovitch rumbled, not unkindly, "Keep your voices down, my daughters." Bluma, his wife, buried her head against his chest. Kiev was quiet again, but the trouble was not truly over. Would it ever be?

*Pogrom.* The dictionary is quite clear on the meaning of the word.

It is a noun which means "an *organized massacre,* especially of Jews." It is a Russian word.

In the Kiev of 1902 and other places, too many places, it meant death, destruction, and the wrecking of human lives. Thus the *pogroms* laid the groundwork for the Holocaust to come.

In the Milwaukee Fourth Street School auditorium, Golda Meir was now surrounded by the admiring children. They had grouped themselves all around her for the question-and-answer session. The atmosphere was one of informality and congeniality. Lou Kaddar smiled her approval. Golda had them all, now. For life.

"Of course," Golda said, in that pleasant voice of hers, "in those days Palestine was ruled by the Turkish government and very few Jews could go there. But human beings just can't live in such terrible choking fear. So my family did what many people of different nationalities were doing then, to escape the persecution and also the poverty of Europe. We emigrated to America."

"How come you picked Milwaukee?" a boy student piped up.

"Well, my father was a carpenter and this was where he found work, I've heard. But I didn't know much about it. I was only eight years old."

Another student, a girl, smiled up at the golden lady. "Did you make up your mind then that you wanted to be Prime Minister?"

"Oh, no. Such a job I never wanted—not even on the day I was elected." She smiled wryly. "I wanted to be a teacher. I thought that teaching children was the finest work a person could do. My parents had other ideas, though. What they wanted me to do was get married."

A murmur ran through the crowd of children.

"Did you have any boyfriends?" It was again the little girl who had asked the question about the Prime Minister's job.

"Certainly I had boyfriends. Why not?" Fondly, Golda Meir remembered. "But somebody came along who wasn't exactly a boy any more. He was older than I was. And he became the most important person in my life."

"Was he nice?" someone asked shyly.

"I thought so. He was a sign painter, when he had work—which wasn't very often. He was the first person I ever knew who really loved things like poetry and music. We used to go to the concerts together—concerts in the park, that is. They were free. . . ."

The years rolled back, scored with lovely

music. Time moved in reverse with lightning speed. The auditorium faded, dissipating into nothingness. Memories, like old photographs which never decompose completely, returned, engulfing her where she sat.

For the listening, rapt schoolchildren in that auditorium, Golda Meir turned back the clock with deft easy strokes, to the beginning again of the time of the first man in her life. The first whole human being, the first soulmate—Morris Meyerson, sign painter, the man who was to join her in her pilgrimage to the promised land. It was not exactly his own idea, though, at the start.

But he was to be the catalyst, the tocsin, the sounding bell, the initial proof of one of Golda Meir's greatest assets in her later life, the very thing that would lead her to the highest hills in Israel or anywhere else: her powers of persuasion, her innate ability to move people. She was never a woman to be denied.

The children of Fourth Street School listened, all eyes, all ears, completely involved, fascinated.

This old woman was a lady who knew how to tell stories.

The sun had been shining that day in the park. The leafy green trees and the glorious grass were a proper setting for the music coming from the bandstand. There, a small but energetic group of musicians was sawing and blowing, filling the area with thunderous music, the music of symphonies, sonatas and fugues. Couples lolled on

34

the grass, listening attentively, fingers entwined, caught up in the melodic sounds which seemed to fill the world of the park.

"Did I hear thunder?" Golda Mabovitch asked from her vantage point on the grass amid a bevy of folding chairs which bore other music lovers. At eighteen Golda was a poised young woman, very attractive and sturdily built, colorful in her red straw hat and ankle-length dress. Her face was aglow with health and radiance.

"Tympany," Morris Meyerson muttered impatiently, as if she were interrupting his enjoyment of the music. He was a tall, slender, angularly built man of somber face and studious mien—an intellectual, clearly, by the look of him. In his pinchback suit, high white collar and bow tie, Morris Meyerson seemed like a man who would amount to something in this world.

"What?" Golda blurted at him.

"Drums. You heard drums. Shhh."

"Oh."

The music cannonaded, thundering upward in a crescendo. The music lovers filling the sloped ground surrounding the bandstand were hushed and reverent, showing their appreciation of the symphonic power. Golda frowned, looking up at the sky. She shook her head.

"I just heard it again. It sounds like thunder to me."

"Sssh," Morris begged her, annoyed. "This is the great *Eroica* by Beethoven."

"This is my new hat," Golda said, firmly. "If it rains the color will run."

"No, no. . . ." Morris shushed her again, in that way of his.

"Yes, yes. The saleswoman warned me. She said, what did I expect, for ten cents?"

"Ssh. I mean, it's not going to rain; that isn't thunder."

"Are you sure?"

"Well, if it is," Morris Meyerson exclaimed in defeat, "God is thundering in perfect time with the music!"

At that, Golda burst into peals of laughter. That elicited many a dirty look from the music lovers around them. Morris Meyerson cringed in embarrassment. Golda had done it again. She was always drawing attention to herself with her uninhibited zest, outspokenness, her blunt candor, saying whatever was on her mind.

Beethoven's *Eroica Symphony* swept to its coda and Morris Meyerson rose stiffly to take Golda Mabovitch's shapely arm and lead her away from the concert. Together, they made a striking couple. But, the music lovers were not sorry to see them leave.

"I apologize if I embarrassed you, Morris. Although it's not my fault you're so witty."

"You really think so?"

"That was an extremely humorous remark."

"Thank you. Maybe I owe you an apology, too. I should have complimented your new hat."

"You really like it?"

"It's very nice. For ten cents."

"Thank you."

36

Arm in arm they strolled along the paved path which would eventually bring them to the entrance to the park. Golda was carrying her precious red straw hat. She had never looked lovelier.

Morris Meyerson, somber expression more intent than ever, spoke first, after a brief, happy silence. There was no threat of rain at all showing in the blue sky.

"Golda, I would like to discuss something with you. It doesn't have to be right now. Let me know when you think it would be a good time to discuss a serious subject."

"Now is fine."

"The subject is marriage," declared Morris Meyerson.

"As it concerns you and me, do you mean?" she asked, without a trace of guile or coquettishness.

"I don't mean President and Mrs. Woodrow Wilson, Golda."

Again she burst into hearty laughter, for he always had that effect on her. His humor was very direct and to the point; unexpected, too. Morris Meyerson, stopping to face her, turned her toward him.

"Golda, I know I don't have a lot to offer, besides a phonograph that could use new needles. But you yourself said it's the first one you ever saw that didn't have a horn."

"That's true," Golda Mabovitch said, quite seriously.

"And I love you, Golda. I love you very much."

37

She looked at him deeply for a long moment, then withdrew from him to sit silently on a bench nearby. Morris Meyerson approached her slowly, thoughtfully.

Golda stared up at him, her lovely face touched with something he had never seen before. "Are you sure you want to marry me? I'm not an easy person. My father says I'm totally intransigent."

"I don't believe your father said that."

"You're right. What my father says is that I'm as stubborn as an ox." She paused. "The reason is, I know what's important to me."

"Well?"

"You are, Morris, dear. I love you, too. You know I love you."

She had lifted up her face to him then and he bent and gently kissed her lips. Then he sighed and sat down heavily on the bench next to her. His somber face was still troubled, still retaining its natural air of seriousness.

"Golda, are you still hypnotized by this romantic Zionist business?"

"I'm going to live on a *kibbutz*," she declared solemnly. "It's a hard life, from what I've heard; even dangerous sometimes. But romantic, it's not."

"Then why get into it?" Morris Meyerson demanded peevishly.

"Because this is the dream that I've had since I was a little girl in Russia, frightened for my life. The dream that we can have the same peace and security other people have. The only way we're ever going to get it is in a Jewish homeland. Oh,

38

Morris—'*If I am not for myself, who will be for me?*'"

"Golda," he railed back at her, "this is America!"

"And I say, God bless America. God bless this beautiful country forever . . . but millions of Jews are not here and never will be. Morris—'*If I am for myself only, what am I?*'"

Morris Meyerson took a deep breath. "Don't you think I'm concerned too? I just don't see that there's any chance for a Jewish state in Palestine at this time."

She restated her arguments. "When was there a better time? When did we have a Balfour Declaration from the British government?" She quoted the words that had burned into her brain: "*His Majesty's Government views with favor the establishment in Palestine of a national home for the Jewish People. . . .*"

"But they don't set a date," Morris Meyerson reminded her sourly.

"Morris," she urged, "'*If not now, when?*'"

"Your friend Hillel didn't know that your other friends, the British, would be fighting a World War and the Turks would be the ones running Palestine."

"But the British will win, and they'll drive the Turks out!"

He stopped trying to dissuade her. "Meanwhile you can't even get there, Golda."

"But as soon as I can!" Her eyes glowed with fervor.

"You're saying that if I don't want to go you

won't marry me?" He could not keep the incredulity out of his voice.

"I can't very well, can I?"

"But if I go, you will?"

"I'd love to marry you, Morris."

"Well, I'm sorry. I'm not going." Morris Meyerson turned away from her in a mixture of rage, futility and disgust. Palestine, always Palestine!

Unhappily, Golda Mabovitch placed her hand on his arm. "I wish you would think about it. Maybe you'll change your mind."

"Not me," Morris Meyerson declared hotly. "Don't count on it. Never."

She glanced at him lovingly despite the utterly adamant expression on his somberly handsome face. She was a young woman in love and he was a man equally in love.

Somehow she knew, in her heart of hearts, that she would get Morris Meyerson to marry her, because she wanted him to. And above all, she would get him to go with her to Palestine. It would be the Promised Land, for the both of them—Mr. and Mrs. Meyerson—the place where Jews would be safe for all time.

The Palestine of 1921 was no different in appearance than it had looked in the time when Jesus Christ had walked the sandy hills. The sand was still there, the dust, the howling winds, the discomfort. To Morris Meyerson and his beloved wife Golda, wheezing along the sandy roadway in a battered rattletrap little bus which looked older than time itself, it appeared that nothing could have changed very much. When they finally saw the chain-link fence, topped with coils of barbed wire, and the clumsily lettered sign which said, in Hebrew and English, KIBBUTZ MERHAVIA, the emotions they felt were a commingling of relief, despair and futility. There was nothing prepossessing about *Kibbutz Merhavia*.

The ancient bus, weathered and creaking, gasped to a halt, engine coughing, brakes squealing on the hard earth.

Morris Meyerson snorted, "I could paint a better sign than that with my eyes closed."

"And you will, Morris. You will."

Together, they stepped from the uncomfortable interior of the dismal bus, taking their few pieces of luggage with them. The bus began to chug away almost immediately, the engine sounding asthmatic as the vehicle labored over the sands. Then the chains on the formidable fence rattled and Morris and Golda turned their attention to that. The chain-link, barbed-wire fence encircled the *kibbutz* completely, like a ring of protective steel. There was a sentry on horseback, with a rifle across his knees, studying them curiously. The man unchaining the gate had a rifle slung over his shoulder. Beyond these men they could glimpse the *kibbutz*. It was no more than a few buildings, mostly small and flimsy, several tents, a water tank beyond the compound, and sand and rocks and more sand and rocks. The horizon was a baked rim in the distance. All in all, it was a thoroughly bleak landscape. Morris Meyerson restrained a cutting remark as he looked at his wife Golda. But she was already concerning herself with the man who had unlocked the gate and was stepping out to meet them. The sentry on horseback had ridden out to look them over, too, at closer range.

"You're the Meyersons?" the man who had unlocked the gate said.

"Yes," Golda said briskly. "This is Morris Meyerson, my husband. I'm Golda."

"Yoel Nesher, Membership Committee," the young man said, eyeing them up and down. "You should have waited to hear from us."

"We waited almost a month," Golda protested. "In Tel Aviv."

"Using up practically all our money, I must tell you," Morris added.

Yoel Nesher showed white teeth in a sun-browned face.

"Well, you could have saved the bus fare out here. Your application was not accepted."

"Not accepted?" Golda echoed, in disbelief.

"I'm sorry." Yoel Nesher really looked sorry.

"Why aren't we accepted?" Golda persisted.

"It's not possible to accept everybody who wants to join a *kibbutz*. Maybe you can get into another one." Nesher shrugged; the matter was closed as far as he was concerned. Morris Meyerson gazed morosely at the old bus disappearing over the sandy terrain.

"What are we supposed to do now?" he complained bitterly. "Walk back to Tel Aviv?"

Yoel Nesher reached down for two pieces of

their luggage, as a gesture of friendship. "We'll put you up overnight. There'll be another bus in the morning." His gaze fell upon the curiously shaped object next to the luggage. "What is this?"

"A phonograph," Morris said coldly. "I'll carry it, thank you."

Yoel Nesher walked off toward one of the crude stone buildings. Golda and Morris Meyerson followed him, their spirits as fallen as their feet. Wind had begun to blow, scattering sand all over the cruel landscape. Behind them the mounted sentry locked the chain-link gate, shutting them in. Forlornly they looked at each other. The wind was hurling gritty sand into their faces. The sentry trotted off on his horse. He had not said one word to them.

Morris sighed. "Well, Golda. You wanted to go to Palestine. We're here. It's enough already. We can go home now."

At that, Golda burst into appreciative laughter and threw her arms around him. Baffled, his arms filled with the phonograph, he could only gape at her in confusion.

"What's that for?"

"For the funniest—I really think so—the funniest joke I ever heard!" With that, she released him and hurried after Yoel Nesher. Morris Meyerson had one moment of total incredulity. Then he too followed, with his phonograph and the rest of the luggage.

Who could argue with a beautiful woman, especially when that woman was a wife? In fact she was your own wife, Golda Mabovitch

Meyerson, who could talk you into desert madness like coming from America, where there was plenty, to Palestine, where there was nothing.

The windstorm rose in violence and strength as the Meyersons began their first day in *Kibbutz Merhavia*. Neither of them realized that it was the beginning of a new life—and perhaps a new ending—for them both.

In their drab quarters that night, the Meyersons had done the best they could to make themselves feel comfortable and at home. The room was plain enough, the Lord knew, but Morris Meyerson was determined to have peace of mind. He lay on one of the two cots provided for sleep, his eyes closed, listening to his phonograph. The Prelude, Chorale and Fugue by Cesar Franck filled the little room with beautiful music. Golda was sitting in a folding chair before the crudely made wooden table in the center of a rather Spartan chamber. She had changed into a clean white dress and busied herself with several pamphlets, looking through them with grim purpose and the sad realization that she had erred badly.

"There's Degania," she said. "There's Ayalet. Where did I get the idea that this *kibbutz* was the best one?"

Morris surrendered. "You were probably right. At least they know their business here."

"Why do you say that?" She looked up from the pamphlets in surprise. He had opened his eyes and was staring up at the ceiling, hands locked behind his head.

"Because any *kibbutz* that admitted me to membership would be out of business in no time." He paused. "You're not laughing, Golda." The strains of Cesar Franck music filled the brief silence.

"It's only because I'm thinking some very serious thoughts."

"Such as?"

"How lucky I am to have you. Who else would struggle halfway around the world to a place like this, just to make me happy?"

Morris Meyerson chuckled goodnaturedly. "As long as one of us is happy."

"Morris, darling—" She left her pamphlets and came to him, then. "You know how much you love me? I love you even more, because you're nicer than I am."

She put her arms around his neck, lifting her face to his for a kiss. There was an interruption, a long peremptory knocking on the door to their quarters.

"I knew it!" Morris sighed again.

"What—"

"The perfect end to a perfect day—they object to music."

He got up from the bed, an angry expression on his lean face, walked to the door, and jerked it open. He found a young *kibbutznik* couple standing there, a man and his woman. They had the typical openness and somewhat aggressive friendliness of all Jews everywhere, who had learned to fight for life's basic needs and com-

forts. Later Golda and Morris were to learn that
their names were Miriam and Reuven.

Morris Meyerson glared at them. "Well?" he
said, challengingly.

"Well, yourself," Miriam snapped. "Would it
bother you to leave your door open, please?"

"Open?" Morris did not understand.

Reuven smiled. "So other people can hear the
music too?"

Morris looked at Golda in surprise and a little
shock.

Golda was equal to the situation. "Morris, ask
them to come in."

Dumbly, her husband stepped back and waved
to the young couple to enter. Reuven, as if on cue,
turned and called over his shoulder down the
hall, "They say come on in!"

It might have been a signal. Now other couples
emerged from their quarters and appeared on the
Meyerson threshold, smiling, eager eyed. Miriam
went directly to the phonograph from which the
lovely music continued to grind out. She stared at
Morris' instrument.

"What kind of phonograph is this? It doesn't
have a horn."

"Quiet, please," her husband Reuven commanded. "Franck is playing. You I can hear any
time."

Golda squeezed Morris' arm joyously, her eyes
shining.

"You see, Morris, darling? You should feel
right at home on a *kibbutz*. That man talks
exactly like you." Suddenly she glanced off and

46

exclaimed in added surprise, "Look!"

At their window, more faces could be seen, more people crowding closer to look and to listen. Morris Meyerson was baffled. Golda was not. "Won't you please come in?" she called out.

In no time at all, more than a dozen people were shoehorned into the tiny Meyerson quarters enjoying the musical interlude. The enthrallment was almost total. The *kibbutzniks* began to keep time to the music, their faces wreathed in smiles. Morris Meyerson was shaking his head when Yoel Nesher appeared and beckoned to him and Golda to join him in the hallway. The Meyersons worked through the packed throng. Yoel Nesher, as young as he was, was still a very military man. His khaki jacket, as well as his bearing—which was thoroughly regimental—set him off.

"Listen, you Meyersons. The Membership Committee has just reconsidered your application."

Morris blinked. "How come so quick?"

"I'm the chairman."

"We're accepted?" Golda marveled.

"On probation," Yesher said. "For three months. Then we'll see."

"We appreciate this, Yoel Nesher. Thank you."

"You're welcome, Golda Meyerson."

He marched off down the hallway, but they could see he was keeping time with the music that was filling the night. Suddenly Golda remembered, and gasped: "Oh, Morris! The quinine pills on the table in the dining room—did you take one?"

"Of course not. Neither did you. We were leaving in the morning."

"But now we're not leaving!"

Morris shrugged. "So? We'll take the pills in the morning. You think we'll get malaria between now and then?"

Golda was adamant, and purposefully efficient. "I don't know, but I'm not taking any chances. You go back to the music. I'll bring us the quinine."

She was off and running before he could stop her, down the hall and out into the desert night. Morris Meyerson smiled tolerantly and returned to the music lovers who now filled his new home. Another of his records had been put on. The strains of a Chopin Nocturne filtered into the close atmosphere. Morris Meyerson began to hum aloud.

Out in the compound area, Golda Meyerson, trying to find her way in the dark, saw the lights in the windows of the mess hall. She hurried toward this, her white dress a flashing beacon in the darkness. She could still hear Chopin behind her, but she was not prepared for the abrupt, spiteful sound of a rifle shot splitting the vast stillness of the night and a male voice bellowing, "Get down, you fool!"

She could only stand still, confused, frightened, at a loss. That was probably why the man's figure came hurtling out of the darkness, slamming her to the ground with a rude thrust of his arm as one more shot crashed in the night. But the man was shielding her as he lay across her, his arm and shoulder protecting her. A horn, a klaxon of some kind, blared raucously in warning and alarm. It was joined by another, and another. The night came alive with tumult.

"You get hit?" the man barked gruffly as he assisted her to her trembling feet. Golda shuddered in the gloom, straightening her dress.

"Just by you."

"Dumb luck. Don't you know better than to cross the compound at night, wearing white?"

"I just came here today. What was that?"

"Arab snipers," came the answer, softer this time, more lenient. "What did you think the barbed wire and guns were for?"

"Now I know," Golda replied simply.

"Here, put this on."

She stared at this new man as he pulled off his khaki jacket and began to help her into it. Even in the darkness she could see that he was very tall and strong looking, a strapping young man. Efraim Ben-Ariel could have posed for the posters that in later years would come to portray the archetypical Israeli warrior, one of those who fought for their homeland and the right to live on it against all odds. The klaxons had shut down now and there was a new silence.

"There probably won't be any more shooting tonight. You can go back to your room. But you might want to think it over about staying here."

Without replying or giving him another look, Golda set off once again in the direction of the mess hall. Efraim Ben-Ariel shouted after her, "That's not the way to your room! Where are you

49

going?"

She turned at that and faced him squarely. Her expression was something he was never going to forget.

"I'm going for quinine."

Golda Mabovitch Meyerson stalked off toward the mess hall. On that night, a leader, a fighter, a giant, had been born. Only Efraim Ben-Ariel and the desert night bore witness.

The Fourth Street School auditorium was a mass of quiet children. Mrs. Golda Meir paused in her story and smiled gently.

"I should tell you what a *kibbutz* is. It's a community of people who live and work together and who eat together in a common dining room. The children are cared for together in the *kibbutz* nursery. Nobody owns anything by himself; together they own everything. And in those days the work was mostly agricultural."

"Mrs. Meir." The principal, Mr. Macy, spoke up from behind the mass of children surrounding the old woman seated on the platform. "The students might like to know how a *kibbutz* got its land."

Golda Meir nodded, agreeing with the thought. "The land was bought from the Arabs—every foot of it—with money contributed by Jews all over the world."

A child in front of her held up a hand, no longer timid. "Why didn't they want to accept you and Morris?"

Golda Meir smiled. "I was told much later that

they thought an American girl would be too soft to do the hard work on the *kibbutz.*"

Another student called out, "How come they changed their minds?"

"That I was never told," Golda answered, "but I always had the idea it was on account of Morris' phonograph."

Another student, as fascinated as the rest of them, murmured, "Was it real hard work on the *kibbutz* like they said?"

"Oh, boy, was it!"

None of the children laughed when she said that, nor did Mr. Macy, the assistant principal or Mrs. Lou Kaddar.

Golda Meir went on to tell of life on a *kibbutz.* It was not exactly two weeks in Hawaii or Disneyland, or a quiet country home in Connecticut—not at all. It was a life right of the days of the pioneers, with perpetual danger the daily ration—the curse of a tribal desert existence.

The Holy Land revisited, by a people who wanted to stay there forever, not go there just for a holiday. God's truth, Golda Meir!

## *Life*

Morris Meyerson was swinging a mattock in the blistering, scorching heat of a desert day. The sun was merciless; so was the assignment Morris has been given by the *Kibbutz Merhavia* Committee. "You will clear the rocks from the ground, Meyerson. Do a good job." It was clearly not a task for a man who loved music, who liked to create with his hands and use his brain. Morris Meyerson was not used to hard physical labor. The mattock, pickax that it was, seemed to weigh a ton. The rocks beneath the hard earth seemed to weigh more than twenty pounds each. The wheelbarrow provided to cart away the cumbersome objects was only half filled now, though Morris had been working all morning long. The sweat stood out on his lean face like so many glistening beads. He was bone weary, heart weary and mind weary. The Arabs could have this land! In Morris Meyerson's mind it was a shout of scorn, defiance and disgust. Golda and her notions! Finally a pesky twenty-four-pounder was vanquished and Morris staggered toward his wheelbarrow, lugging it painfully.

It seemed ages before the barrow was at last filled. The sun had moved in the azure-blue sky. Morris Meyerson, aching, every bone and muscle crying out in protest, tried to raise the barrow to carry off the rocks to their destination. But handles defied him as he lifted. The rock load was far too heavy. He struggled valiantly with the wheeled contraption toward a pile of rocks. He had to lose; it was inevitable. He did. The heavy wheelbarrow toppled sideways and the load spilled with a crash. Morris fell too. Embarrassed, he gazed about him. Had anyone seen his stupidity, his weakness?

Some distance off, other working *kibbutzniks*, toiling with spades, shovels and rakes, witnessed Morris Meyerson's defeat. Their derisive grins were visible to him.

He cursed long and hard, but he rose to try again. The hot sun mocked him. It was a torment.

Golda Meyerson was no less unhappy with her chores that day.

In one of the outside kitchens of the *kibbutz*, she had been assigned to pluck chickens. They had parked her on a stool in one corner of the little room and left her with a pile of the filthy, feathered things. Golda hated this job. She could not hide the disgust on her face as she plucked away. Her eyes showed her misery. She was perspiring copiously in the close heat of the kitchen. And just when she had plucked clean the last chicken in her assigned pile, a woman came in with another basket heaped with more chickens. Golda gazed in dismay, her heart sinking as the woman dumped the feathery load at her feet. Chicken plucking in Palestine—was this the way to freedom, salvation and the road to tomorrow's statehood?

It did not look like that from where Golda Meyerson sat.

In the *kibbutz* meeting room that night there was a *cumsitz*—a discussion get-together attended by virtually all of the forty members of *Kibbutz Merhavia*. The meeting room was actually the mess hall, with all the tables pushed aside to the walls and the attendees sitting on chairs and the floor. At one end of the hall Yoel Nesher sat with the other officers of the *kibbutz*. In his role of chairman he was pointedly official.

"Next on the agenda is the question of whether or not to hire outside labor."

Golda Meyerson was startled into sudden awareness. The handsome young man seated next to Yoel Nesher was very familiar to her now. But Morris Meyerson, plainly bone weary, was hardly paying attention to the proceedings. He could have cared less.

"I call on Efraim Ben-Ariel," Yoel Nesher boomed.

The strapping, good-looking, powerful Ariel stood up. He seemed a giant.

Golda tugged at Morris' arm. She was really impressed. "Oh, look, Morris. That's him!"

"Who?" Morris yawned, blinking.

"Efraim Ben-Ariel, the man who kept me from

getting shot!"

Efraim Ben-Ariel seemed to have a good memory, too. Even from where she sat against the back wall with Morris, Golda could see his brief smile and nod as his eyes fell on her before he began to speak.

It was a warm smile, a smile that welcomed. Even a foolish woman who ran across the compound at night in a white dress so that Arab snipers could get a crack at her.

Golda listened raptly as he spoke, her eyes glowing. But Morris Meyerson had all he could do to keep awake. He was very tired.

The *cumsitz* moved along. Ariel made his report, gave his opinion. The *kibbutzniks* clapped their hands. Ariel sat down.

Golda Meyerson looked on, watching, listening, and learning a great deal.

Morris Meyerson dozed.

Poor darling, Golda thought. He tried so hard.

In the *kibbutz* fields, they gave Morris Meyerson a team of horses and a plow and told him to go and make the land fertile. Morris tried, as God was his witness. With the leather reins draped about his neck and his two hands wrestling with the handles of the plow, he tried, both industriously and valiantly. The horses lurched, Morris pushed, the plow dragged fitfully, with spasms and jerks. The animals kept going with the forward movement of the plow. Morris tried to keep pace but it was no use. He fell down in his very tracks, his long face buried in the sand and mud. He might have suffocated if Reuven and Nahum, seeing his plight, had not come on the run.

Grinning and laughing, they pulled him to his feet.

"What the matter, Morris?" Reuven chided him. "Don't those mules go for an American accent?"

Then Nahum stopped laughing. "Hey, take a look at him."

Morris Meyerson, mud stained, defeated, was shivering as though from cold, despite the beads of sweat dotting his lean face.

"Are you all right, Morris?" Nahum peered up at him. He brushed gingerly at the mud caking Morris' face.

"I'm just fine," Morris Meyerson said.

Reuven looked skeptical. "You sure?"

"Who can be sure of anything here," Morris retorted, "until a committee says so?"

They had no answer for him as he gamely mustered his strength, shook off their helping hands, and plodded back toward the horses and the bothersome, difficult plow. Nahum and Reuven exchanged glances.

Morris Meyerson gathered up the reins again, grimly, and grasped the plow handles. He called out to the horses to get them going.

He teeth were chattering and his lean body was trembling.

Nahum and Reuven, who had returned to their chores, did not see that.

In the *kibbutz* kitchen not far away, Golda,

Rachel and Gabi were busy, too. Water was running noisily from a tap in the sink, raising a cloud of spray. The women were washing big pots and clanging and banging them angrily. At least two of them were: Gabi and Rachel, Golda's helpmates, were vocal in their disapproval of what they were doing. Golda had become fairly good friends with these two *kibbutznik* women; people in the same boat tend to get along. That is not only the way of Palestine, it is the way of the world.

Rachel's sneer was mighty. "I thought this was a progressive *kibbutz*. Ha-ha. It's positively Victorian. Woman's place is in the kitchen."

Golda refused to accept the bait. She had her own ideas. "I saw women in the olive grove."

"But you never saw a man in here," Rachel snarled.

Gabi laughed. "You want to know when you'll see men on kitchen work? When we get women on the assignment committee."

Rachel bitched further. "Gabi, I'm sick of it—so sick I'm telling them tonight that they'd better put me on something else!"

"Tell them in terms of a specific assignment," Gabi suggested.

"Livestock," Rachel said. "Even poultry."

Golda was amazed at that. "Really?"

"Yes, really. What's wrong with that?"

"Why would you rather feed chickens than people, Rachel?"

Both women stared at her, surprised. How did one answer that? Meanwhile, none of them had noticed that the sound of running water had ceased. Gabi mopped at her sweaty face.

"That's a funny way to look at it. Nobody likes working in the kitchen. I know I don't."

Golda smiled. "I don't exactly love it either. But I love chickens even less. I think I'd be afraid to be alone in a room with a live chicken." She shivered as if cold.

"You mean," Rachel asked, "in America there are no chickens that aren't cleaned and plucked?"

They all had a good laugh at that, even Golda. And then Rachel noticed the trouble with the faucet. "Oh-oh, the water's off again. I'll go find a man." She left the room. Gabi and Golda toweled at their perspiring faces. The steam still clung to the atmosphere.

"What's the trouble with the water, Gabi?"

"The valve is clogged."

"Is it hard to fix?"

"They just hit it with a hammer."

"Then why do we have to find a man?"

"Because the valve," Gabi explained, "is on the roof!" She pointed upward. "High up. Are you going to climb up there?"

Golda frowned, but only for an instant. Gabi continued, "Besides, we don't even have a hammer."

But she was talking to Golda Meyerson's back. Golda had already left the kitchen to see for herself. Up above, squinting against the sunlight, she saw the small water tank on the roof, with its pipe that led down to the sink in the outdoor kitchen. For a moment she pondered. She had no hammer—but then she spied the clutter of tools on the ground nearby. There were shovels, rakes, hoes, but still no hammer. She picked up a shovel, gauged the distance to the roof and then tossed it to the top, where it landed with a noisy clatter. Close to the building was the wire enclosure that was the chicken coop. Shutting her mind to the clucking, smelly fowl running around behind the enclosure, Golda put her hands on the wire mesh and raised herself from the hard ground. She began to climb. It took all of her resolution and nerve, but she was not going to wait for any man to do this job, when a woman could do it too.

The wire fence sagged alarmingly with her weight, but she went up anyway—strongly, assuredly, purposefully. The chickens squawked and gabbled at her presence above them. Golda Meyerson climbed. It was high.

She reached the edge of the roof and pulled herself to a firmer footing. There was the thrown shovel, waiting for her. Walking gingerly across the roof, shovel in hand, she reached the valve. She gave it the flat of the shovel in a determined whack which rang like a bell.

Turning, she called down to Gabi, "Try it now!"

In the kitchen, Gabi turned on the sink faucet. The water hissed and flowed steadily. Wonderingly she sang out, "You fixed it!" Miracle of miracles. . . .

Smiling, contented, Golda Meyerson began to climb down from the roof again, using the wire fence for a ladder of descent.

60

Rachel had not yet returned with a helpful man. Score one for the women of *Kibbutz Merhavia*.

Rachel came back with Efraim Ben-Ariel before Golda had reached the ground. Ariel frowned, pointing with his hammer at the descending figure.

"Who is that up there?"

Rachel looked up in wonder. "The American girl." Her tone was sour.

Efraim Ben-Ariel smiled, his swarthy face admiring.

He liked Mrs. Meyerson a great deal, liked her more the more he saw and heard of her. She was what Palestine women should be. Bless them all. She was needed in *Kibbutz Merhavia*, for a fact!

That night in the *kibbutz* meeting room, a session was well underway. It was a meeting of the committee, with Yoel Nesher in charge, as was his duty. Also present were moody Rachel, Miriam, Nahum and Efraim Ben-Ariel, as well as a few other members of the *kibbutz*. Rachel had the floor now as Chairman Nesher presided with an authoritative air.

"I have no objections to him. He does the best he can. But I have serious doubts about her. She would turn this *kibbutz* upside down if we give her the chance."

Yoel Nesher asked, "Can you be specific?"

"She's already trying to institute hot cereal for breakfast," Rachel exclaimed triumphantly.

Nahum was aghast at that—alarmed, even. "Do

61

you mean, instead of herring?"

Rachel folded her arms. "That's just one of her ideas."

Miriam raised her arm. Nesher said, "Miriam?"

"I'm going to be honest," Miriam offered. "This is a personal attitude I don't expect anybody else to share. I can't stand her ironing dresses."

"I share it," Rachel said. A murmur ran around the room. The men looked puzzled. Yoel Nesher spoke for all of them.

"Explain that, please."

"The rest of us, when we change clothes for dinner, we go to the laundry, take a clean, folded dress off the shelf—and that's good enough for us. She—she had to *iron* her dress."

"I see," Yoel Nesher said thoughtfully. "Anything else?"

Miriam interjected, "Sometimes she wears stockings to dinner."

Everybody was silent then, particularly the men. They were gravely weighing these charges against a new member of *Kibbutz Merhavia*. The committee clearly had its duties, its responsibilities.

Then Efraim Ben-Ariel spoke his mind. All listened; he was an admired man, honored by more *kibbutzim* than this one. A leader.

"The established tastes and attitudes of the group are very important. We have to be careful not to be too severe, or too lenient, either. On balance, therefore. . . ." His smile was truly glowing. "I say she's an absolute joy to have around."

Every man in that room, which served as mess hall and meeting room, said in chorus: "So do I!" Rachel and Miriam took their defeat bitterly, with the jealously of women who had already sensed the difference and the greatness and uniqueness of Golda Mabovitch Meyerson. That was why they had tried to rid themselves of her forvever. But the men of *Kibbutz Merhavia* could not be denied.

Mr. and Mrs. Meyerson stayed on, thanks to the intercession of Efraim Ben-Ariel.

A word from him was law in Merhavia.

The Meyerson bedroom was without music, for once. Morris, lying on his cot, dressed except for shirt and shoes, was reading from a slim book. He looked fairly well, considering all he had gone through. Golda, in her pale slip, was brushing her hair with short, rhythmical strokes of a caramel-colored brush.

Morris was reading aloud: "'And thou beside me, singing in the wilderness—Oh, wilderness were Paradise enow.'" He closed the book and looked at Golda. "How did Omar Khayyam know to write this for me personally?"

"You're glad, aren't you, Morris?"

"Certainly. I'm glad to still be alive after three months of this place. A summer resort it's not."

"You can joke. But you work hard. You made them respect you. And now we're *kibbutzniks.* You should be very proud."

Morris Meyerson sat up in bed, dangling the hand holding the book over one angular knee. His expression was genuinely fervent. "Golda, darling, I *am* proud—that I have you. I've always been very proud of you."

She came to sit on the cot with him, forgetting her lovely hair in her sudden flush of quiet happiness. She kissed him and smiled. "*Kibbutzniks.* We don't own anything. We never will. And yet we own all of Merhavia! The land, the fruit trees—everything is ours!" She laughed, a little-girl laugh. "Doesn't it make you feel rich?"

"So." He smiled, too. "What can we afford now? A Pierce-Arrow automobile?"

"I was thinking of a baby," Golda answered, in a low voice.

The silence was long. Morris' tone was very hard when he finally replied, "I didn't hear that."

"I'm saying we should have a child now."

"Is that right? Well, when did the committee tell you we can go to work on this child? What night? What hour?"

"What committee?" She did not understand his abrupt rage.

"How can we do it without instructions from *some* committee? Isn't there a committee to regulate *everything* around here?"

He had sprung erect from the cot and turned upon her, openly angry for the first time in their relationship. "No, Golda! No baby! Not now!"

Stunned, hurt, she could only murmur, "Well when, then?"

"I'll tell you when! When we're living someplace else, not here!" He was quivering with his anger now, towering above her. She stared up at him, thoroughly demoralized.

"Why, Morris?" she begged. "Why?"

"Because I will not have my child raised by other people, fed and washed and held, not by his parents but by someone else! Put to bed not in our home, but in a nursery with strangers! The baby wakes up crying in the middle of the night and who comes to him? A committee!"

She watched him, shocked, as he raged on, setting his bare feet into the shoes by the cot. "No, thank you," Morris Meyerson roared on, "if I'm going to be a father, I want to *be* a father, not a visitor!"

"So." She controlled herself. "Where are you going?"

"Out. Because I know you're going to try to talk me into this, like you do everything."

"I would never do that. Not to you—and not to the baby." She smiled at him tenderly. "All right?"

"All right." He had calmed down as suddenly as he had previously flown into a rage. He started to take off his shoes again. Golda turned out the light in the little room, plunging them both into darkness. The sudden silence and gloom were heavy. Golda began to take off her slip. Morris was undressing in the vicinity of his own cot.

"Considering this discussion, Morris, you won't be angry about what I have to do?" she whispered in the darkness.

"What do you have to do?" he grumbled.

"Well, now I have no reason not to agree to what they asked me."

"*Who* asked you?"

She was pulling on her nightgown. He could see her shapely outline in the gloom. Actually, he knew what she was about to say.

"A committee. They want me to go to Haifa for a month to take a management course."

"If you want to go, go."

They got into their own cots and pulled up the blankets. The desert night outside was calm and peaceful. The war had been waged in here this time.

"Good night, Golda," Morris said, softly.

She heaved a long, long sigh. "Good night, Morris." It was a sigh only another woman would have understood.

"I see you feel bad about the baby," Morris said. "I'm sorry."

"There is no baby to feel anything about. I was thinking of the course."

"What kind of course?"

"How to raise chickens."

Morris Meyerson could not see the acute unhappiness on his wife's face. He had turned over on his side and shut his eyes.

Golda Mabovitch Meyerson slept badly that night. And the next. And the next. Then she was off to Haifa to learn how to raise chickens. For the good and well-being of *Kibbutz Merhavia*. But the legend that was to be Golda Meir was now truly underway. The greatness had been there from the very beginning, as far back as Kiev, Russia, in 1902, when, even as a child of five, she had demanded to know the answers to all things.

*What is a pogrom?* It was the question her sister Sheyna had never really answered to her satisfaction. Neither had anybody else, for that matter.

Months later, there was something to celebrate in *Kibbutz Merhavia.* One night in the mess hall-meeting room, now converted to party festivity, all the *kibbutzniks* reveled. Morris Meyerson's amazing phonograph, set up on the table, was blaring forth with a wild and chaotic *Hora* and all the members of the *kibbutz* were dancing energetically to the gypsy fervor of the music. Everybody was having a fine time. Reuven and Miriam led the way, reeling, turning, twisting expertly to the melody that will set anyone of Jewish stock to dancing. Golda and Morris were vibrantly alive, hands locked, cavorting. The meeting room echoed with laughter, joyous shouts, the pounding music. Morris' hornless wonder played on. Golda Meyerson was back from Haifa and Morris was glad to have her back. When the music finally jarred to a stop, Morris, now worn out, gasped for breath.

"That was marvelous!" Golda said, out of breath. "Where did you get that record?"

"Your sister. Sheyna sent it from Milwaukee for a birthday surprise. I'll put on the other side."

"Who wants to be reminded of birthdays?" Golda looked at him fondly. "You'll come back and dance?"

"This one, dance without me." He was fanning himself.

"Morris? Are you all right, darling?"

"Oh, sure I am. I'm not tired." He grinned broadly. "Of course, my horses are exhausted."

She laughed with her usual appreciation of his humor but she watched him concernedly as he walked off the dance floor toward his phonograph. Poor dear, he *did* look tired—worn out, really. The rest of the revelers were having too much fun to note Morris Meyerson's condition. Nor could they see beyond the mess hall walls where, just outside the barbed-wire fence surrounding the *kibbutz*, a shadowy form bearing a rifle crept forward. Then the figure raised an arm as if in signal and another rifle-bearing shadow emerged from the darkness, going toward the enclosing fence. Suddenly the shadows were joined by yet another figure. A shovel shone briefly in the moonlight. The shadows began to dig under the chain-link fence.

Efraim Ben-Ariel, crossing the darkened compound toward the sounds of laughter and music, did not see the shadows either. He came into the mess hall, eyes searching the happy dancers. When he saw Golda he strode purposefully in her direction. The new record was beginning to turn. Dancers were choosing partners. He halted Golda before she could step on the floor again. In his khaki jacket and boots, he had never seemed taller or handsomer. When he loomed before Golda, he smiled.

"How about taking a break? I need to talk to you about a couple of things." His voice was firm, yet low and confidential.

"But the dance—"

"We will have the next one. Come."

He took her hand and led her away from the music. She fell in step with him, unused to an authoritative male. Papa Mabovitch, bless him, had been very soft-hearted. And Morris—Morris was, well, Morris. Efraim Ben-Ariel was a man of a far different stamp.

"First your chickens," Ariel began smoothly.

"Let's talk about the other thing," she said dryly.

"The finance committee just went over the books. For the first time poultry is showing a profit. Not only that—it's the biggest profit of any of our operations."

"As you once said to me, Ariel . . . dumb luck."

"Not luck at all. You're an extremely capable person. Whatever you do, you do well." He searched her face with his keen eyes. "So we want to send you to be a delegate to the *Histadrut.*"

If the *hora* had left her breathless, this was even more stimulating. "Oh, no. Not me. I couldn't. . . ."

"It's only a labor union," he said gently.

"It's *the* union!" she protested. "It's as big as . . . as a government! I wouldn't know what to do!"

"I'll give you a few pointers. I'm a delegate, too. Come with me, Golda. I won't let you refuse." His eyes bored into her. She couldn't ignore his tone, nor could she ignore the look on his face. His eyes were clearly hinting at some deep inner personal feelings. Golda was all too aware of it. She hesitated.

"Ariel, my Hebrew is bad."

"Speak English," he commanded. "They'll listen. You have a way of putting things that makes people listen."

She might have argued further, she might have protested anew, but suddenly, abruptly, with a terrifying speed, the klaxon alarm system set up all around the *kibbutz* went off, blaringly loud.

"What's that?" she gasped, clutching his arm.

Efraim Ben-Ariel shook his head. His face was a rigid mask.

"Go back to the others. Tell everybody to stay put and turn the lights out. Hurry."

She raced back into the mess hall just as searchlights crisscrossed their beams in the darkness, picking out the small buildings, the water tank. Nothing else was visible save the sand and the shadows.

Ariel called out: "Nahum! Over here!"

Nahum came on the dead run, a rifle at high port in his hands. "Raiding party," he blurted.

Ariel nodded. "How big?"

"Don't know yet."

"After the livestock?"

"Looks more like they're after us; they're headed straight this way!" He gestured and Ariel could now see the shadowy invaders—there seemed to be a horde of them—coming slowly across the compound area. He pushed Nahum ahead of him into the mess hall and quickly padlocked the big door. The *kibbutzniks*, huddled and silent now, the music at an end and all the lights out, waited in the darkness for the trouble that was coming. There were flashlights and lanterns but Ariel held them in abeyance. The air was hushed. The room was tense; no one dared to breathe. Efraim Ben-Ariel took quiet command, as was his way. He had lost sight of Golda Meyerson, but it didn't matter right now.

"Let's all stay calm," he ordered. "We've lived through these things before. Who's assigned to guns this week?"

Several of the crouching men raised their hands. The last of the hands going up belonged to Morris Meyerson.

"Go get the guns and bring them here. Understand? Here. Noplace else." The men sprang to do his bidding.

Morris looked at Golda in confusion. She stared at him. "What is it, Morris?"

"The phonograph—" he said thickly.

"I'll take it," Golda snapped. "You get the gun!"

As she raced off, Morris blinked. He was shivering uncontrollably again. Efraim Ben-Ariel did not see his condition. He was too busy taking charge of a very dangerous situation.

Outside, the shadowy figures of men had begun to crawl through the cut portion of the fence. In the light of the moon they looked ominous, deadly. Their very silence was terrifying.

Efraim Ben-Ariel waited, with his people, for the onslaught. The one thing a Jew living in Palestine had to live with every day, every moment, every second, was attack by those who would prefer them dead.

Morris Meyerson, out of breath, pawed at the padlock on the small cupboard in his and Golda's living quarters. By the light of a lantern he sought the old double-barreled shotgun stored there, and a bag of cartridges. His hands were not quite steady. The alarm horns still blared all over the *kibbutz* compound. When Golda entered the room carrying his precious phonograph, Morris was breaking open the shotgun and stuffing the barrels with shells. But his hands were shaking so badly he dropped several of the shells. Guiltily he flung a look at Golda. The paleness of her face and her shocked eyes startled him.

Golda murmured, "Something is wrong."

"Nothing is wrong!" he blurted angrily. "Nothing, I said. What are you staring at?"

He was shivering violently—that she could see, dim as the light was. She crossed the room, reaching for the shotgun to take it from him. He pulled away from her.

"Let me have that, Morris."

"I can handle it."

"No you can't! You're shaking."

For a moment they wrestled for possession of the weapon, in a mad lurching stumble about the room. Morris panted, crying out desperately as they struggled, "I can still do what I'm supposed to do!" He recoiled from her, holding the shotgun.

"You won't make it across the compound, Morris. It's an Arab raid! Please, darling—"

"This is my job!" he shouted. "My job! Don't

you dare take over!"

"They need the gun! Please, let me bring it to them!"

Finally Morris Meyerson, weakened, distraught, could not match her strength. He lost his grip on the weapon and tottered to the floor. Without wasting another second, or paying him any attention, Golda picked up the shotgun and the scattered shells and ran out of the room.

Morris Meyerson lay trembling on the floor, gasping feverishly.

Outside, Golda loaded the shotgun as she ran. The searchlights were poking frantically again, illuminating the darkness of the night. The alarm horns were louder than ever, blasting away. She did not see the thin cord stretched at ankle height across her path. When she tripped on it, she uttered a low scream and pitched headlong on her face, losing her grip on the shotgun. She reached for it again, frenziedly, only to have a heavy boot, a man's boot, clamp down on the weapon very heavily.

"Don't try it," a thick voice rumbled from above her.

She raised her head to stare, frightened beyond fright.

Three men were surrounding her—booted, armed, rifle-toting men who looked like Death itself. She tried to rise. One of them had scooped up the shotgun. She tried to speak. No words came.

And then the voice said, "You can get up now. It's all over."

"What?" She rose to her feet uncertainly. "What's all over?"

"The exercise," the speaker grunted. "We're the *Haganah*."

Golda Meyerson's mouth hung open in amazement.

The man handed her the shotgun, his smile grim and humorless. "Next time, sister, you won't be so lucky. If there is a next time for you fools."

Floodlights came on. The entire compound was lighted like day. Ariel and the *kibbutzniks* had poured from the mess hall, shouting and angry. There were more than a half dozen of the *Haganah* invaders herding them into the middle of the compound. Even without uniforms of any style or conformity, the *Haganah* men looked like Arab attackers. They all wore the kefiyah, the Arab headdress, and their faces were blackened. The horns had cut down. Efraim Ben-Ariel stormed to the fore venting his anger. "I want to know who's in charge!"

The man who had spoken to Golda stepped forward.

"I am. My name is Yuval. I'm a sergeant."

"What the hell kind of exercise do you call this, Yuval?"

"A totally unauthorized kind," Sergeant Yuval replied easily. "Be a good fellow and don't report it. I could lose my stripes."

Nahum, at his wit's end, protested aloud. "Why train *here*?"

Yuval shrugged. "Naturally, a proper training camp would be better. The trouble with that is, if

74

the British catch us at it, we'll do our next exercise in prison. We're not allowed to exist, remember?"

Efraim Ben-Ariel was helpless. So were the rest of the tired and frightened *Kibbutzniks*. Sergeant Yuval had spoken nothing but the truth. With his mock raid the point was well taken: had they really been Arabs, *Kibbutz Merhavia* would be a charnel house now. The security and protection systems would certainly have to be improved.

The *Haganah*—the unofficial fighting arm of the Jews in Palestine—was technically an outlaw band of soldiers, those Jews who chose to bear arms and fight for their rights—and their survival. There was more than one Sergeant Yuval in their ranks. Ariel knew the breed and admired them, in spite of everything.

"No, Sergeant Yuval," he said crisply. "We will say nothing of this raid. We're foolish enough, as it is."

Yuval and his men smiled.

All Jews were brothers, no matter what.


Morris Meyerson was in bed again, warmly covered with blankets, ministered to by a very penitent Golda. She sat on his bed, smoothing his blankets, patting his pillow, all love and concern. The incident of the shotgun that night lay between them like a cloud.

"Why didn't you tell me?" she asked forlornly.

"I didn't want you to worry. It's only vivax malaria—that's the mildest form."

"Oh, Morris, how do you know?"

"I read up on it in the library. It comes and goes. I figured if I take enough quinine, one day it will just go."

"Doctor Meyerson, I presume."

"You can say that again, Golda. Because I know the cure for what ails me." He sighed and stared up at her. "I'm leaving the *kibbutz*."

Her reaction was a shocked silence. She tried to smile, to shake her head at him.

"You don't mean that. You're just saying it because you're sick."

"No. I made up my mind last night."

She flared up at that, angry, hurt. Her eyes misted. "Why? What is it—pride? I didn't want to take the gun! I had to! You see that, don't you, Morris?"

"It wasn't the gun," he said, calmly enough, in spite of her agitation. "Not exactly. The gun just showed me once and for all that I'm not the right person for this kind of existence. I can't handle anything about it." Suddenly he cried out, desperately, "Golda, I don't want to spend my life feeling sick and useless!"

She bit her lower lip, controlling herself and the war inside herself. "Where do you want to go?"

"Depends on you. If you'll come with me, I'll stay in Palestine. If not I'll go back to America."

Golda was silent now but her face expressed her agony. Morris reached for her hand. "I know you don't want to leave the *kibbutz*. But I didn't want to leave America. You asked me then to change my mind. Maybe you'll change your mind this time."

She stroked his fevered forehead slowly, gently. "Morris, darling, if you're leaving, I'm leaving. There's nothing to change."

She bent to him, kissing his cheek, resting her face against his. She had to do that. She did not want him to see the tears welling up in her eyes. Golda Mabovitch Meyerson knew her duty to her husband Morris.

There was no celebration when they left *Kibbutz Merhavia*, no flag waving, no shouting, no gifts. But in their own way the *kibbutzniks* made the Meyersons know how much they would be missed.

SHALOM, GOLDA AND MORRIS read the banner on the chain-link fence the morning the Meyersons, bags packed and ready, waited for the same old minibus to take them away. And the phonograph, too.

Nahum was there, and Reuven and Miriam, Rachel, Gabi, Yoel Nesher and Efraim Ben-Ariel. Their faces wore smiles but their eyes held a great sadness. Morris pointed proudly to the new sign on the gate which clearly had been done professionally: KIBBUTZ MERHAVIA.

"At least I painted them a better sign, didn't I?"

"You certainly did." Golda squeezed his arm.

"I should have painted that one, too," he added, indicating the crude SHALOM, GOLDA AND MORRIS banner. Golda laughed. Morris and his sense of humor—she would always love that about him.

The wheezy, ancient bus rattled in from the distant horizon. The sun glared down as always. The desert sands seemed serene, lovely, for once. The Meyersons reached for their luggage, the very same they had come with. Everyone moved forward. The men took the luggage, over Morris' protests, and stored it in the bus. Rachel, Miriam and Gabi all embraced Golda wordlessly. Tears filled Golda's eyes. The men all put their arms around her, too. Efraim Ben-Ariel looked at her in a way she would never forget. Then he too turned away, without a word. But his touch had spoken volumes to her, his eyes had said much.

The Meyersons boarded the ancient bus sadly, quickly.

Before it could pull away, Morris Meyerson cried out, "Hold it! Hold it just a minute, please."

The bus door swung open again. Morris emerged, carrying his precious hornless phonograph. He handed it to Reuven with a brief, "Here," and then ducked back into the bus. The vehicle wheezed asthmatically again and lumbered down the roadway. Reuven and the kibbutzniks stood dazed and silent watching the Meyersons go out of their lives, perhaps forever. Reuven clutched the phonograph dumbly.

Far off now, almost out of sight, the bus became a tiny dot on the desert landscape, merging with the scenery.

Another chapter in the life story of Golda Meir had closed.

Only life itself would open the book and turn the pages again. It was a life which still

had agreat deal of living to do—an enormous
amount.

# *Death*

The deeply interested children in the Fourth
Street School auditorium gazed unblinkingly at
the golden old lady seated on the platform before
them. Mrs. Golda Meir had paused in her wonderful story, to fill in with some footnotes to the
exodus of the Meyersons from *Kibbutz Merhavia*
in Palestine, that desert home for homeless Jews
where fruit trees grew only because Jews had
planted them.

"So we left the *kibbutz,* which I was very
unhappy about. And we went to live in Jerusalem
. . . and the years passed. Morris became a
bookkeeper, and I became the mother of two
children."

"What were their names?" a girl student asked
quickly.

"Our son's, Menachem. Our daughter's, Sarah."

The children all smiled. A boy called out, "Did
you like Jerusalem?"

Mrs. Golda Meir's half smile was wistful as
she remembered.

Jerusalem. The Arab market, lined with stalls that sold all things to all people, Jews or not. The Moslem women in their traditional cover-up clothing, the veiled faces, coming to the marketplace to pick at the produce filling the stands; their men, wearing the *kafiyeh* headgear; British policemen, unmistakeable in uniform and bearing, watching the streets like bulldogs ready to spring. The Jerusalem of 1928, an unhealthy interest of the United Kingdom, was ever a trouble spot on the globe. As if the infernal heat and the Arabs were not enough—

"Well, Jerusalem is a wonderful city. But Morris' wages were terribly low and there was never enough money to feed the children. Not in those days, my little friends. I have to say that those years were the worst years of my life."

It came back to her at that moment, the whole terrible day of ordeal. The humiliation, the mental hurt at the souk in Jerusalem, the Old City.

She was carrying her year-old baby and a shopping bag, and now her face and figure showed the passage of time. She had put on a little weight and her face had fleshed out some. But she was still a beautiful woman, albeit matronly now. The baby was heavy and so was the shopping bag, but she entered a food stall. It was like all the others in Arab marketplaces. Meat, fish and poultry were displayed on one long table, all of it unrefrigerated. There were bins bursting with vegetables, and packaged groceries on shelves. The shopkeeper, Mehemet, was dark-eyed, reptilian, polite.

"*Salaam aleykum,*" Mehemet had greeted her.

"*Aleykum salaam,*" she had responded, looking at his wares.

"I have nice fresh fish," he continued in Arabic. "Do you care for fish?"

Golda smiled, tiredly. "I'm sorry, but you just heard all the Arabic I know."

His smile was tolerant. In broken English he replied, "You like chicken?" Golda had drawn closer to inspect one of her old nemeses.

She nodded. "How much is chicken today?"

Golda could not afford the kosher prices—humiliated by poverty, she shopped in the Arab quarter.

"That one, sixty *piastres*. Special to you."

"Give me about twenty *piastres* worth."

She moved away, as he readied her purchase, selecting staples for the Meyerson household—pita bread, rice, eggplant, condensed milk. The baby squirmed in her grasp, making it difficult. When she got back to Mehemet her chicken was ready and he was ready to tally up her purchases. His eyes gleamed happily. Golda saw the pile of oranges close by and lingered for a second, debating her choices. "Lovely oranges from Jaffa," Mehemet crowed. "Full of juice."

"No, this is all I need."

"One pound ten." Mehemet rubbed his hands.

Golda fished in her purse for the money while he placed the items in her shopping bag. When she handed him a bill, he frowned as she said, "Ten *piastres* . . . and this is a pound."

"This is not a one-pound note," he disagreed.

"Of course not. It's Credit Union scrip."

"I don't take it." Mehemet shook his head vigorously.

"Everybody takes it," Golda protested. "My husband works for the Credit Union and this is how they pay him half the time."

"Madam," Mehemet said patiently, "I know why you come to me instead of the Jewish shops—because you owe them money and they won't take your scrip."

Golda was becoming upset. Her face paled, her chin quivered. "Look, I can't afford to feel insulted. I've got two children and no food at home. You've taken my scrip before. Why won't you take it now?"

Mehemet snarled, "I have to pay a discount to get rid of it!"

"I'll give you an extra ten *piastres* to make up the difference!" Golda was desperate now, feeling trapped and helpless. "That's all I have!"

Mehemet stared at her in obvious disbelief.

"Is that all right?" she persisted, putting the money on the counter again.

Mehemet showed his teeth in an angry grimace. "No, madam, it is not all right!"

"It will have to be!" she shouted back at him, almost out of her mind with worry and exhaustion. The baby squirmed again in her arms, about to cry. "I told you I have no food for my children!"

Without saying more, she lugged her baby and her bundles out of Mehemet's shop. He blanched at the defiance and then yelled, "Stop! I will call the police!"

But Golda Meyerson kept on going, heedless of his shouts. He ran to block her, now screaming hoarsely in Arabic, "Police! Police! Somebody call the police!" He was waving his arms wildly, outraged.

In moments a crowd of robed and trousered Arabs had appeared, collecting at the mouth of the stall, directly in Golda's path. All were gesturing and taking up Mehemet's cry for help. For Golda the mad moment was just too much. She wheeled, taking her baby and her bundles to the rear of the stall, away from the screaming mob, and sat down on a box of some kind. She began to weep in sheer misery, hugging the baby to her. Mehemet was appealing to the crowd for justice now, explaining his case. Crying fiercely, Golda did not see the man in the business suit who had witnessed her attempted flight and now stood before her, looking down, with a kind expression on his handsome face. He was a man she would have recognized in a million men.

"Hello, Golda," a familiar voice said softly.

Golda's head snapped up. Now she was truly embarrassed.

"Oh, my dear God. Ariel!"

Efraim Ben-Ariel's presence at such a scene was almost a mockery to her. She tried to dry her eyes, brushing at them though her hands were full of baby and bundles. She began a rush of questions to keep him from doing the same. His kindness only made her feel worse.

"How are you, Ariel? What are you doing here? Did you leave the *kibbutz,* too?"

"No, I'm sort of on loan to the *Histadrut*. I've been in Jerusalem for a year. How about you?" His words were easy, his manner calm, just as it had always been even at the worst times in Merhavia.

"Oh, I'm . . . fine," she murmured, despairingly, emptily.

"And Morris?"

"Fine, fine, no more malaria. And how is your wife? I heard you got married."

"Yes, to Gabi. You remember her from Merhavia."

"Of course I remember Gabi." The pot-and-pan washings, the faulty valve on the water tank that day—Golda shook herself.

"She's very well," Ariel went on, as though they were not surrounded, literally, by an Arab merchant and his friends, crying out for justice and cash and police. "Where are you working, Golda?"

"I'm—sort of retired."

Ariel seemed shocked. "You're not working?"

Some of her usual fire came back, in spite of the mess she was now in. "I wouldn't call taking care of two small children loafing."

"I wouldn't call it anything much, considering how badly we need your capabilities," Efraim Ben-Ariel answered cuttingly.

Mehemet's Justice had finally arrived. Two British policemen materialized, threading through the Arab throng. One of them came directly forward to Golda and the expostulating Mehemet.

"What appeahs to be the difficulty heah?" The officer, Sergeant Leigh, had a thick accent.

Ariel smiled. "No difficulty, Sergeant." He had stepped between Golda and the officer, gesturing to Mehemet as he dug into a pocket of his coat.

Ariel spoke warmly to Mehemet. "My friend, will you accept a pound note in exchange for that miserable Credit Union scrip?"

Mehemet beamed, his troubles at an end. He did not like trouble. "With pleasure, sir."

Golda watched admiringly as the exchange was made. Sergeant Leigh and his colleague moved off, seeing there was no need for them. Mehemet spread his arms, indicating to Golda that she was free to leave. She glared at him and pushed her way out to the baby carriage. Ariel followed, smiling. He joined Golda as she thrust the carriage forward down the souk street, narrow and cobbled as it was.

Mehemet came dashing from the shop, calling out, "Madam!"

Golda and Ariel stopped and turned. Hurrying toward them was Mehemet, bearing two golden oranges.

He held them out to a bewildered Golda, muttering, "*Salaam aleykum?*"

The question held in the hot atmosphere. For a long moment Golda struggled with the temptation to tell him what he could do with those oranges. But then wisdom prevailed. "*Aleykum salaam,*" she said politely, and accepted the peace offering.

Efraim Ben-Ariel chuckled deep in his chest.

"You're a born diplomat, Golda Meyerson," he said.

Menachem Meyerson, the infant son in Golda's arms, gurgled as if in agreement.

It is a wise baby that knows its own mother.

By the light of a kerosene lamp Morris Meyerson washed his hands in a bowl. Golda was at the wood-burning stove, stirring the contents of the pot cooking there. The stove needed more wood and she popped in another stick. The Meyerson home—an apartment, actually—was a miserable, cramped place, in many ways meaner and less pleasant than their quarters at *Kibbutz Merhavia*. Morris Meyerson had much on his mind, since Golda had come back from shopping with her tale of meeting Efraim Ben-Ariel and receiving his offer. It was something to think about. Anything was, where Golda was concerned—his Golda.

"What kind of a job would this be—part time?"

"No. Full time," she answered simply.

"Can you handle a full-time job and everything else?"

"I have no choice; that's the job—secretary of the Women's Council. It is no small thing."

Morris dried his hands with a linen towel. "Ariel must be a big man in the *Histadrut* if he can offer you something like that."

"They need someone who speaks English fluently," Golda said, not wanting to talk or think about Efraim Ben-Ariel.

Morris sat at the table. Golda served him a bowl of hot soup. He broke off a chunk of the pita bread on the table and began to eat in silence. She knew him very well, knew he did not like the idea of her working. She also knew that soon he would argue about it. So she waited, bracing herself.

"The job is in Tel-Aviv, Morris."

Morris Meyerson looked up from his soup, spoon poised. "Well, he's got a helluva nerve, trying to talk you into Tel Aviv when I work in Jerusalem."

"He didn't have to try very hard, Morris. I took the job."

He put his spoon down noisily, speechless. He blinked.

"Eat your soup while it's hot," Golda said.

"Never mind the soup!" he bellowed at her.

"You wouldn't say that if you knew what I went through to get a piece of chicken for it."

"Golda!" He stared at her, incredulous. "What are you going to do—walk away from me? Walk away from the children?"

She tried to smile. She could not. "Of course not. The children will come with me."

"Who will take care of them all day while you're working?"

"My sister will help. My mother and father are coming next month. I'll get very good babysitters through the Women's Council—" She trailed off lamely, for she could see the fire in his eyes.

"You've got it all figured out, haven't you?"

"Yes, Morris. I have."

"So what have you got figured for *me*?"

"A job in Tel Aviv," she explained, "as soon as we can find one."

"And in the meantime?" His tone was sharp, edged.

"You could visit us on weekends." That came out of her timidly.

Morris Meyerson almost wrung his hands. "Oh, Golda, tell me it's not definite. Tell me you won't decide all this without even discussing it."

His plea was too late and not good enough. She had drawn herself erect, steeling herself against feelings of frustration and guilt.

"No! I've discussed enough!"

"With whom?" he demanded angrily.

"With myself! How many years am I supposed to throw away on fighting with storekeepers? I came here to work and build a homeland! That's not something I just feel like doing—it's what I started out to do with my whole life. And nothing's going to stop me any more!"

Morris Meyerson was silent, head bowed, knowing all too well that he could not stop her— never, in a century of trying. Almost contrite, Golda sat down next to him, softening in guilt, knowing all too well what she was doing to him.

Morris smiled bleakly. "I should have gone back to America while I had the chance, before the children were born."

"Morris—" She touched his hand. "Don't feel that way. Please give things a chance to work out for all of us. I'm going to try very hard to make them work. I promise you."

Morris Meyerson was staring down at his soup. It was cold now, but for want of something to do, he resumed eating it slowly, very slowly. There was no more to be said. Golda had said it all—as usual, as was customary in the Meyerson household.

Mrs. Lou Kaddar, on the platform with Mrs. Golda Meir that day in the Fourth Street School auditorium, could have spoken for her here. She knew the Golda story very well, especially the Meyerson part.

"It was some years before Golda could bring herself to face up to the failure of her marriage. But at this point, it was as good as finished."

Yet Golda could speak for herself, as she always had. "There is a type of woman who cannot let her husband and children narrow her horizons."

The children kept on growing, no matter what happened between their father and mother. Nature cannot be stopped. Pictures flashed through Golda's mind.

Sarah, lovely Sarah, in her crib, smiling and babbling.

Menachem, handsome boy, a toddler already, taking big steps.

Sarah crawling across the kitchen floor, eyes shining.

Sarah, age three, in her best dress, the gingham one.

Menachem blowing out the four candles on his birthday cake.

Menachem, age six, catching a candy-striped ball.

Sarah at five, dressing her favorite doll.

90

Menachem, eight, Sarah, six, playing together with their pile of wooden blocks, two little ones in harmony.

In her new position as secretary to the Women's Council, there were letters to write, lists to make up, minutes to report and, of course, articles to author. Golda Meir could always write.

"When such a woman becomes a working mother, her inner struggle with guilt is sometimes more than she can bear. I remember my own feelings all the time my children were growing up, and even afterward. I would wonder, 'What do they feel toward me?' 'What do they really have in their hearts?' Because there's no doubt that I neglected them, although I did my very best not to be away from them one extra hour. And I always provided capable people to take care of them."

Cheery, efficient babysitters watched Menachem and Sarah, but always Golda felt a sharp sense of guilt as she went to kiss her children goodby before leaving them with the sitter for the day. The march to the front door was an ordeal.

"There would be a moment when I was going off, leaving my children with the stranger, when they would flash me a look of reproach. Please don't go! Stay with us! That look would go through me like a stinging arrow! That look was almost enough to destroy my whole fine argument and me along with it."

But always Golda Mabovitch Meyerson would go out and shut the door and leave anyway, no matter how much it hurt. She had a job to do, an important job, one that meant the world to her—the Jewish world.

Mrs. Lou Kaddar remembered those years all too well, as who would not? There was the face and figure of Adolph Hitler looming large in the consciousness of the world—the little strutting, pompous Caesar with the outthrust arm and the hoarse, unforgettable voice, enjoining marching legions of goosestepping German soldiers and a cooperating German citizenry to walk him to his destiny. Swastikas and eagles appeared, Germany re-armed in spite of the Treaty of Versailles, and the Hitler War Machine began to roll. Yes, Lou Kaddar—and the world—would never forget the years 1933-39.

"For the next ten years, while an Austrian corporal was coming into power, Golda was advancing in the *Histadrut* to the level of the Executive Committee, presided over by political leader David Ben-Gurion. And then, in May 1939, with World War II less than four months away, Britain issued its controversial White Paper."

The infamous document seemed to sign the death warrant of every Jew living in Palestine. The British stand gave Hitler one more arrow in the attack that would lead to the Holocaust, the horror the world would turn its back on. With the statement of indifference Britain washed its hands of Jewish concern, of humanitarian interest and the Brotherhood of Man.

It was one of England's less shining hours.

The *Histadrut* committee room in Tel Aviv received the teletyped news of England's position in an all-pervading gloom. As Efraim Ben-Ariel read aloud from the yellow transcript, a tense, angry mood dominated the room. Golda Meyerson, David Ben-Gurion and several other officials could hardly credit their ears. But Ariel was reading the damaging words all too clearly.

"His Majesty's Government now declare officially and unequivocally that it is not part of their policy that Palestine should become a Jewish state."

Golda broke in stormily, "How can England just wipe out its own Balfour Declaration that promised to establish a Jewish homeland here?"

David Ben-Gurion motioned Ariel to continue his reading. The little, broad-shouldered man with the thatch of flowing white hair put both hands together in a pyramid of patience.

Ariel resumed reading: "From now on, Jewish land purchases are restricted . . . to five percent of Palestine. Jewish immigration is restricted . . . to fifteen thousand per year for the next five years."

One of the officials, Meged of the heavy, worn face, grunted in disgust, "And after the five years?"

"No further Jewish immigration will be permitted, unless the Arabs agree to it." Ariel flipped over the sheet in his fingers and stared around the table at everyone. Golda returned his stare with a defiant toss of her head, to combat the tears building in her eyes.

"Unbelievable," she exclaimed. "God knows what horrible things that lunatic in Germany is planning for all the European Jews. This is their last chance to escape. Their only real hope is to come here. And this is the time the British Government picks to slam the door in their faces!" She fought back the sob rising in her bosom.

Efraim Ben-Ariel grimly dropped the sheet on the table. His handsome face was stony and unsmiling. "Well. We have to fight them on this, any way we can."

Meged's cynical eyebrows rose. "Fight the British?"

"Damn right," Ariel said fervently.

A murmur ran around the table. Meged shrugged, trying to measure the mood of the room. "Trouble with that is," he said, after a pause, "when the war breaks out the British will be on our side, fighting Hitler. We must be very careful what we propose here."

Now they looked to their leader, David Ben-Gurion. Golda had long admired this strong, patriarchal man who had led since the days of darkness. David Ben-Gurion smiled thinly and unclasped his hands, laying them flat on the table. His voice was steady and calm.

"We will fight this White Paper as though there were no Hitler. And we will fight Hitler as though there were no White Paper."

Golda Mabovitch Meyerson felt like cheering out loud.

With Jews like David Ben-Gurion there was

hope for a future for Palestine—a Jewish future. Golda was proud of Ben-Gurion, Proud that he was a Jew like her.

Fighting the White Paper as though there were no Hitler meant smuggling immigrants into Palestine under the guns of the British destroyers patroling the waters off the coast. And many other undercover, underhanded things.

Golda Mabovitch Meyerson's apartment in Tel Aviv became a very busy place in the weeks and months that followed. For one thing, its small balcony faced the harbor and looked out to sea. There, on many a night, civilians in the guise of house guests and visitors to the Meyerson apartment could station themselves in perfect ease, with binoculars, to check the shipping coming in and going out. Lavi and Arnon, two of the *Haganah's* most efficient men, had this job. Efraim Ben-Ariel was also a frequent visitor to the apartment whose downstairs bell and nameplate read simply: G. MEYERSON. Golda had become indispensable to the plans of David Ben-Gurion to bring Zionism to Palestine.

One particular night a new visitor came to the Meyerson apartment, around suppertime. It was a slender young man bearing a large, heavy suitcase. He pressed the buzzer of Golda's door and a feminine voice from inside asked, "Yes?"

"Hofstaetter," the young man said, shifting his suitcase.

"Open the door and come in," the voice said. "Slowly."

Hofstaetter did as ordered. But once inside, he stiffened and looked amazed. The person who had pushed the door shut behind him was a young girl in her late teens, perhaps, as cute as a button—except for a Thompson submachine gun she had trained on Hofstaetter, cradling the weapon as if she knew how to use it. Hofstaetter blinked.

The girl poked the gun at the suitcase he was carrying. "Is that the radio?"

At his quick nod, she demanded curtly, "Open it and let's see."

Hofstaetter smiled. "You're kind of pretty, you know?"

"Let's see the radio." The nose of the Thompson jerked upward.

He did as he was told. Setting down the suitcase, he snapped open the latches. A short-wave radio, the Hallicrafter type, about 26 x 14, was clearly visible. Efraim Ben-Ariel now loomed in the doorway to the kitchen, studying the young man and the machine-gun-bearing girl. His expression was serious, despite the white apron tied about his trim middle. "Shulamit," he said, softly. "Be a little kinder. The fellow has come a long way to help us."

Hofstaetter grinned at that and bowed to the girl. "Hello, Shulamit."

"Hello," she said, and then smiled and lowered the gun.

Ariel turned back into the kitchen, where Golda was taking a hot pan out of her oven. She set it down on a small table and began to beat the contents of a bowl. "The radio operator is here," Ariel said. Golda nodded. "Would you scoop out the eggplant for me? Careful, it's hot." Smiling, he walked toward her. The affection on his handsome face was there for all the world to see. He opened a side drawer and produced a metal cooking spoon.

"No, no, Ariel. Not with that spoon. A wooden spoon."

Efraim Ben-Ariel did as he was told.

In the living room, young, serious Hofstaetter set up his radio. He took a long antenna wire and walked it out to the small balcony, where Arnon and Lavi were studying the shore with their binoculars. Hofstaetter dropped the antenna wire over the lip of the balcony.

Lavi looked at him, lips pursed. "We have an incoming vessel, the *Delos*. Tell her to alter her course north. A British destroyer is patroling here, too close."

Hofstaetter shrugged. "*Delos,* eh? A Greek ship?"

"It should only be a ship," Lavi said sadly. "It's an interisland ferry."

Hofstaetter completed his necessary arrangements, returned to the living room and stationed himself at his suitcase radio. Taking up the key, he began to tap out his Morse signals. Shulamit, still holding the gun, watched him as he worked, with a mixture of curiosity and feminine interest. Hofstaetter, mindful of her presence, kept on sending.

In the kitchen, Golda had readied her bowls of

food. Ariel had the pita bread portions. "I'll take it out to them," he said.

"Then tell Shulamit to come eat. The child looks pale."

That amused Ariel. "What are you, mess sergeant to the whole *Haganah*?"

Golda Mabovitch Meyerson paused to look at him. "She's my friend Esther's youngest daughter and like a niece to me."

Efraim Ben-Ariel had no more arguments for her.

He found Shulamit sitting with her tommy-gun across her lap in the darkened living room. Ariel smiled at the girl. "She says come eat. The child looks pale."

"Can't eat 'til I'm relieved," Shulamit said.

Ariel chuckled. "I relieve you, pale child. Hand over the tommy-gun." She handed the weapon to him with a grateful smile.

He was checking the chambers expertly as she went into the kitchen.

Shulamit ate the way the young usually do, with zest and a hearty appetite. Golda brought her a tall glass of milk as she scooped up her *tahina*, that delicious dip that tasted so grand with the pita bread. Golda did not notice that Shulamit was looking in the direction of the living room where Efraim Ben-Ariel was spelling her.

"Very nice, I must say," Shulamit remarked.

"You like the way I make *tahina*?"

"Your *tahina* is nice, too. I was talking about Mr. Ariel." Mischievously, Shulamit twinkled at the older woman. "What's your secret?"

"A dash of *cayenne* pepper," Golda said.

"And what's the secret of you and Mr. Ariel?"

Golda Meyerson looked puzzled.

"Come on, Golda, everybody's talking about you two."

Golda took a moment to answer that one. After all, she had been honest all her life. Why stop now? And Shulamit, young as she was, was a woman. She was the right age to understand about men and women, the birds and the bees, and life itself.

"Let them talk. What would be wrong? You know the old Yiddish saying, '*Mein neshuma is nisht a rozhinka.*'"

"I don't understand."

Golda Mabovitch Meyerson made an elaborate explanation. "Oh, I beg your pardon. I forgot that *sabras* don't care to learn Yiddish." She smiled. "Rough translation, '*A person is not a stick of wood.*'"

Shulamit laughed delightedly, though covering her mouth quickly to stifle her mirth. Golda was reminded so much of herself as a young woman that she had to smile back.

As young and possibly virginal as she was, Shulamit the *sabra* understood. Raised since childhood to carry a gun and learn how to fight for her homeland, she had not had to be taught about men and women. And in this terrible day and age, a woman had a right to find any happiness she could. A man, too.

To Shulamit, Golda and Mr. Ariel were two of

the finest people on God's earth—giants, really.

It was wonderful that they could make each other happy.

Shulamit was a very intelligent young lady.

Fighting Hitler as though there were no White Paper, as David Ben-Gurion had said, meant working with the British military, providing Jewish parachutists for missions in occupied Europe, training as many Jewish soldiers as the British would permit.

Hitler's armies had marched into Poland, occupied Paris, taken over the Continent. It was now Fortress Europe. And Great Britain, the last holdout against Der Führer's blitzkrieg might, was fighting for its very existence, its life. The darkest days of the war were going on now.

Despite the White Paper, Britain tended to be very lenient toward Palestine, the Jews and the Zionists. But they still had not relented enough.

By God, they needed the Jews—every last man of them, and woman too.

Particularly Golda Mabovitch Meyerson.

## *Adversities*

On an infiltration course hidden in the desert, Major Orde Wingate was putting his Jewish trainees through their paces. Major Wingate was one of the most respected of the British military in Palestine. He had supervised the entire training program for these Jewish troops—light explosive charges, simulated mortar fire, a machine gun that kept up a chattering fusillade, all of it. And he exhorted his trainees in that British way of his, "Straightaway, now! Good chaps!" Today twenty soldiers were responding to Major Wingate's very British technique of instruction. The major himself was setting off the detonations. At his side, another officer was traversing a machine gun, rapidly pocking the earth and air with deadly bullets as the twenty soldiers crawled forward on their faces and bellies. "Come straight on!" Wingate bellowed cheerily. "Good chaps! And keep those tails down!"

Major Orde Wingate was a slender, wiry man in his forties. The big Webley revolver on his hip and the uniform and its rank were the marks of the soldier, but the mark of him as a man was the slightly mad gleam of the happy warrior in his eyes. Next to him, lying on the ground working the machine gun, was Moshe Dayan, wearing a special type of uniform which included an Australian Army type of hat. Major Wingate, who was to become world famous himself, liked Moshe Dayan of the *Haganah*—liked him very much.

The training cadre was a great success with the help of such a man.

"Okay, lower your fire!" the Major ordered crisply.

"Lower, sir?"

"I want those men to feel the breeze of the bullets!"

Dayan stopped firing, unable to go on. The crawling troops, his own Jewish compatriots, had already had a pretty hard time of it. "Major Wingate, the bullets are coming pretty close now."

Wingate, speaking quietly, in his customary gentlemanly manner when not issuing orders, said, "No fear. You can't possibly hit your men."

"Ummm—how is that, sir?"

"The Lord is fighting for the children of Israel," Wingate said, quite seriously. "Are you familiar with the Book of Joshua, Chapter Ten?"

Dayan promptly quoted: "'Then spoke Joshua, "Sun, stand thou still upon Gibeon. And thou, Moon, in the valley of Aijalon."'"

"And what was the result?" Wingate smiled

grimly. "The sun stood still and the moon stayed until the nation had defeated its enemies. And there was no day like this before or after. For the Lord fought for Israel. Have I quoted correctly, Dayan?"

"You certainly have, sir," Dayan said.

"I suggest then that you Jews would do well to put your trust in the Lord as much today as Joshua did in his time."

"We'd better," Dayan agreed grimly.

"Then be good enough," Major Orde Wingate suggested, "to lower your fire."

Moshe Dayan grinned widely. "Yes, sir!"

Tapping the gun mount, lowering the barrel and the sights, he resumed firing, kicking off a blistering hail of lead. The troops crawling forward hugged the earth as the murderous fire blasted overhead, very close to their flattened forms, their faces dug into the dust.

Moshe Dayan marveled at Major Orde Wingate. How could one not like a man who knew one's Bible better than one himself did?

"Come on, chaps! That's the ticket! No turning back now!"

Joshua fought the Battle of Jericho in Biblical times. Moshe Dayan and his men fought the Battle of the Infiltration Course in the infernal desert heat. In the beginning, before the big battle, the important one, came at long last.

Golda Mabovitch Meyerson came on an official visit to see Major Orde Wingate in his tent on the training camp grounds. The portable military desk in the major's quarters served as their conference table. Golda was pleased to meet the major. This meeting was long overdue; Moshe Dayan had been singing the praises of Wingate for months.

"Major Wingate, it isn't just that everybody tells me you're a fine officer and a wonderful man, they say you may be the only British officer who thinks very much of us."

Wingate waited for her to say more. He had heard much of this extraordinary woman, but he had not realized that she was also so attractive. Mrs. Meyerson had very compelling eyes!

"That's why I'm going to ask you if you can tell me what kind of plans your generals have for our soldiers."

He made a bold, swift sketch on the notepad before him, to help answer her question. He was a good hand with a pen. "The present situation in North Africa is this: the Germans are threatening to take Egypt by storm, seize Cairo and then invade Palestine, which is why our top brass decided to train a Jewish contingent here."

"But they will only train five hundred men," Golda protested. "How can five hundred stop a Panzer division?"

Wingate spread his hands. "The intent is to form them into sapper teams to blow up bridges and so on."

"I see," she said, defeated. "Tell me, do you think the Germans will get here?"

"I'm quite sure they will not," Major Wingate said very seriously, "if only because of overextended supply lines. They'll be stopped well short of here, Mrs. Meyerson."

"And if that happens, what becomes of our training program?"

"That's easy. The brass will stop training Jews a damn sight faster than they started. Forgive my language."

Golda admired his bluntness, his directness.

"Major Wingate, you are supposed to be training five hundred men, so naturally you'll train only five hundred. But it could be five hundred at a time, then another five hundred."

Major Orde Wingate's eyes lit up with fire. The woman was talking his language. He had always appreciated cleverness, tactical brilliance, stealing a march on the other fellow.

"That is a positively smashing idea!" he ejaculated.

"You wouldn't object?"

"Mrs. Meyerson, I won't be here much longer. I'm being posted to Burma—the Burma-China-India theater of war. Therefore—" his very blandness was a tonic to Golda—"while I'm still in the land of Israel it is my duty to help the children of Israel make the most of the opportunity God has given them."

"Wonderful!" Golda exulted, but then her face clouded. "But there's the problem of inspections. They'll come around and see it's not the same five hundred men."

"I'm sure they'll never notice at all."

"Why won't they?"

Major Orde Wingate smiled, a strange smile.

"Because, as some of my classmates at Sandhurst might say, all you people look alike to us. *Hah!*" His humor was typically British, hearty and zestful.

Golda Mabovitch Meyerson laughed along with him, from the bottom of her heart. Would that all British officers were like Major Orde Wingate! *He* was the opportunity God had given the children of Israel. He was a good man with the power to make use of his goodness.

Golda had to restrain an impulse to reach across the portable military desk and hug him. Major Wingate was a *mensch,* a true *mensch.* A *man.*

In April of 1945 German concentration camps were liberated by victorious Allied soldiers, who have never been able to forget the horror of what they found and what they saw in those terrible places. Death camps and their survivors were something new to the Twentieth Century—Auschwitz, Buchenwald, Dachau, Bergen-Belsen, Treblinka, human beings reduced to walking skeletons, massed corpses stacked in common graves. The barbed wire, the watchtowers, the ugly tents and the crematoria stacks poking into the skies over Germany and Poland. No, nobody would forget the outrages the Nazis had committed as they "solved their Jewish problem" by abandoning every decent human code of behavior.

Yet when the war had been over for a full year, some of those homeless walking skeletons who had survived were still in a concentration camp. This one was ringed by British barbed wire, and was on the island of Cyprus. There tens of thousands of frail survivors, intercepted while trying to reach Palestine, were quarantined and stored, packed in like so many cattle in the Quonset-type huts in the burning sands. There the D.P.'s—the Displaced Persons of the earth—looked out at their captors and wondered if the war, repression and cruelty were truly over after all. How many Hitlers could the Jews take in one lifetime? No one could say for sure.

Golda Mabovitch Meyerson saw the dream coming, the Jewish dream which burst into flames after the war, during those terrible days when Jews waited interminably in Cyprus prison camps. What else could a Jew call them?

"When did the idea of an independent Jewish state change from a distant dream to an immediate need? It was when we Jews in the land of Israel, six hundred thousand strong, found ourselves helpless to rescue our own people because of the policy of an occupying foreign power—the British Government. That's when we learned we had to take our future into our own hands."

Golda Meyerson went to Cyprus as an official of the Jewish Agency to plead with the British commissioner, Sir Stuart Ross, to save the children imprisoned in the Cyprus camps. It was a job she understood and undertook with all her heart.

Sir Stuart Ross was a middle-aged civilian

with a kind, gentle appearance. The several medium-rank British officers accompanying him and Golda Meyerson as they toured outside the Cyprus internment camp, were clearly nonsympathetic to the sight of the prisoners beyond the wire enclosure. But Golda ignored them. Sir Stuart was the man to appeal to. He had the power, not these uniformed jackals.

"I'm only talking about the young children, Sir Stuart."

"How young?" His manner was courteous, courtly, considerate.

But she could see that his eyes were troubled as they scanned the frail inhabitants of the Cyprus camp—particularly the children.

"Under the age of one year. The doctors say most of them won't live through the winter in this camp. Isn't there some way to give them priority to leave Cyprus and go to Palestine?"

Sir Stuart Ross shook his head. "The British Foreign Office is a stickler for its own rules. And the rule at this camp is: first in, first out."

Golda Meyerson shuddered at that. It could be a death sentence. "Sir Stuart, you and I have had a lot of dealings in Jerusalem. In my opinion you're much too decent to let children die for a rule like that."

Smiling, Sir Stuart Ross studied her admiringly. "I knew what I was up against when I heard Mr. Ben-Gurion was sending you. You are a formidable person, Mrs. Meyerson."

The inspecting group reached the gate, where everyone paused. "Mind you," Sir Stuart Ross conceded slowly, "only these very young children." He gestured at some of the small pinched faces staring through the wire fence at the visitors. They stared back curiously, a little frightened.

Golda cut in, "And their parents. If they have parents left alive. You can't separate them, naturally."

"Naturally." He had barely hesitated, for as she had said, he was a decent man. "But you do understand this will have to be done under the regular immigration quota. The number going out will have to be subtracted, Mrs. Meyerson."

She nodded, happy that she had won a small victory.

"And," Sir Stuart continued amiably, "those who are waiting to go in turn will have to agree to let the others jump to the head of the queue. You agree to the fairness of that?"

"I made arrangements to talk to some of the leaders," Golda said. "And now you know why Ben-Gurion gave me this job."

"Why?" the good Sir Stuart Ross wanted to know.

"Nobody else would touch it," Golda Mabovitch Meyerson answered. She continued walking out the gate. Sir Stuart Ross chuckled appreciatively and followed in her wake. The junior officers fell into step behind them. The inspection tour was over.

But another victory had been won—a Pyrrhic one, true, but a victory all the same. Now it remained to win the agreement and approval of those Jews stuck behind the wire walls of the Cyprus camp. That would not be an easy thing, for people who had suffered so much for so long. To give up your chance to go to Palestine, even for a small, helpless child, could be asking too much of any Jew who had nearly died under Hitler's rule.

Stoller put it, perhaps, best of all.

Stoller, a gaunt man with burning eyes, whirled on Golda Mabovitch Meyerson when she made the proposal to a dozen or so half-starved refugee wretches crowding the Nissen hut that day. There were women among those pitiful wrecks, too, Minna and Leah. The men were named Aronowitz, Lenski, Hazan, and, of course, Stoller. Hazan was the oldest, but Stoller was the most vocal in his outrage at Golda's plan.

"One year I'm rotting in this place! One whole year! You trying to say somebody who came last week should go ahead of me?"

"I'm saying, a child, yes," Golda said firmly.

Minna clutched at her pitifully thin breasts, her eyes haunted pools. "I'm sick myself. If I stay much longer I'll die here."

Golda tried to ease her mind. "We're trying to get you all out. But the children first."

Aronowitz looked at her with a great sadness.

"Please, I understand about the children. But their parents don't mean anything to me."

"*Children* don't mean anything to me," Leah shouted, her savage face a mockery of womanhood. "I can never have any. Would you like to see

110

what's tattooed on my arm, Mrs. Meyerson?"

The bitter tears that suddenly erupted from her were like a tidal wave of emotion. Golda was shaken by the sight, unable to keep talking.

Lenski, so thin he was almost skeletal, asked softly, "I'm on the list for next month. Are you asking me to wait another year?"

"Oh—" Golda tried to rally. "It won't be that long."

"How long?" Minna wailed. "How long?"

Stoller sneered mightily. "It could be forever!"

"No, no," Golda answered, miserable now. "Why?"

"They say soon the British will stop sending us to Palestine altogether!" Stoller told the room at large, with mammoth belief. The hut now became a scene of great agitation. The woman wailed and wrung their hands, the men appealed to some higher power.

And then Hazan, the eldest, raised his arms for silence. "Quiet!" he intoned commandingly. "We are people, not animals! We are still people!" The hut stilled as though some messiah or holy man had appeared in their midst like an apparition.

"My dear madame from the Promised Land," he said quietly to Golda, "every captured ship is a separate camp here. Every camp has its own committee. We are not authorized to act for all the others." It was a point well taken, one that must be considered.

Golda Mabovitch Meyerson responded to that—as she always did when the chips were down, the issue was in doubt and something

111

constructive simply had to be done. She put aside her pity and fears and said quite calmly, "Would it be possible to call a meeting of all the committees?"

It was possible.

Stoller, Lenski, Aronowitz, Minna, Leah and all the others could do nothing but agree to a meeting. It was a way of doing *something*, much better than simply arguing.

Hazan, like the wise sages of old, had shown the way.

Golda Mabovitch Meyerson faced them all, the committee people, later that afternoon. They pushed their way into the Nissen hut, filling every available inch of space, to hear her, this golden woman who had been so important to the Jewish cause since the beginning.

They sat on the bare ground or leaned against the walls of the hut, and they all listened to what she had to say. They listened so intently that one could have heard the beating of their hearts. But Golda's words rang louder.

"I could say that the children are the future of any country. But let me speak of the present. The Jewish children of Palestine—the *sabras*—are a miracle." Her tone was reverent. "How I wish you could have seen them on the beaches, meeting the ships that managed to get through! These children—sixteen, seventeen-year-old girls and boys, with no memory of persecution, no experience of suffering—risked their lives to jump into the waves and carry the Immigrant Jews ashore."

112

She paused to hold back the sobs in her words, her tone.

"Some of the survivors told me they cried for the first time, after all they had been through. This was what made them shed tears—the children helping them. If you could have seen these blessed children of ours! I know you would want every child here to have a chance to grow up like them, erect and confident, strong, and pure as the sun of Palestine."

There was no more she could stay.

She ended her speech and, composing herself, quietly left the hut. They all let her pass. Minna and Leah were crying openly. The men had knotted their hands in prayerful clasps and Hazan was staring up to the roof of the hut as though he were seeing the messiah. The emotional spell in the Nissen hut was mammoth.

Golda Mabovitch Meyerson had had one more golden moment, in a lifetime of golden moments. But where would this one lead?

When she emerged from the hut, shaken, in a turmoil of heart, mind and soul, wondering what would come of her talk, it was to find herself surrounded by a flock of children. Each of them seemed to be holding something behind their backs. Golda, puzzled, stopped.

"*Shalom!*" the children chorused, as one.

And with that they thrust out their hidden hands. A surprise! In each was a paper flower, grotesque, pitiful, beautiful.

"*Shalom,* children." Golda knelt to the sand,

accepting the drab, poorly made paper flowers. To her they might have been orchids. "Oh, what beautiful flowers!"

The oldest boy, David, smiled happily. His companions clapped their hands. "You like them, Mrs. Meyerson?"

"Thank you, thank you." The tears were not far away. "Where did you get them?"

"We made them," David explained proudly. "Our teacher from the land of Israel showed us how."

Golda Meyerson trembled, trying to smile. "You know, in the land of Israel we love flowers very much. On every Sabbath table, maybe there are candles, maybe not; there may not even be a lot to eat. But there are always flowers."

The smallest girl came forward timidly. "Is this what flowers look like? I never saw a real one."

Golda Meyerson took a long moment to absorb that awful truth. And then Hazan the Elder emerged from the hut and quietly motioned her to join him. Golda rose to her feet, smiling her goodbys to the children. Hazan smiled a little too, sadly. His expression was prophetic.

"Well, we voted," he said simply, as they halted a few paces from the children. Golda stared at him, waiting.

"And—"

"And by a big majority, the children can go first."

"My dear friend, thank you."

Golda Mabovitch Meyerson could say no more. She walked away, trying to keep her shoulders from heaving, to hold the fierce sobs of joy in check. She was not successful.

She had to lean against the base of the watchtower close by to support herself. Her legs felt like rubber. She looked at the paper flowers in her hand and suddenly she was weeping heartbrokenly, no longer the staunch, unbeatable Golda Meyerson.

A moment passed—an eternity of tears, a lifetime of regret.

Sir Stuart Ross materialized abruptly behind her. His voice was gentle, tender.

"Mrs. Meyerson, you mustn't cry. You can be very, very proud of your people. They have nothing left in the world but a place on the list, and they've given that up for others. It's to the everlasting credit of the human race, Mrs. Meyerson. Why should you cry?"

Golda raised her head proudly, but the tears would not go away. "I'm crying," she said, "for the children who never saw a flower, Sir Stuart."

Weep, world, weep, too. Cry, Golda, cry. Such monstrous things had become possible in the Twentieth Century, thanks to hate, bigotry, slaughter, wholesale insanity and antisemitism, that blight of the Jewish heritage which had put an entire people behind an eightball that was almost two thousand years old.

Lake Success, New York; the United Nations, a noble experiment.

November 29, 1947: forty-five years after that night in the Mabovitch home in Kiev, Russia,

115

during the *pogrom*. The United Nations, on this day, voted on a recommendation of its own committee that Palestine be partitioned into an Arab state and a Jewish state, with Jerusalem internationalized.

Golda Mabovitch Meyerson could hardly envision a Jewish state without Jerusalem, and there were many other things she felt were wrong with the United Nations proposal. But the UN plan had to be accepted. Partition was much better than nothing. One step at a time, that was the way. Partition first, and then—

Golda would never forget that fateful day. "We were all glued to the radio, of course, following the UN vote with pencil and paper—yes, no, yes, no. Ten countries, including Great Britain, abstained. Thirteen, including all the Arab countries, opposed. Thirty-three, including the United States, voted in favor."

And that same night, in a radio studio, Golda Meyerson of the Jewish Agency gave the speech that made her personal star shine even brighter than before, that made her name even more of a Palestine legend than it was already if that were possible.

"As of midnight, local time, we have the right to be a state." Her audience could not see the emotional rapture on her face. "On behalf of the Jewish Agency, I will say something to our Arab neighbors. You have fought your battle against us in the United Nations. The majority of the countries in the world believe that this is now as it should be. It's not what you wanted. It's not what we wanted. It's a compromise. Now we say to you: A Jewish state can be a great benefit for everyone in the Middle East. We hold out our hand to you. Let us live together in friendship and in peace."

Her voice trembled slightly, but only because her emotion was heartfelt, honest, completely genuine. All of her listeners that night heard her emotion, including the Arabs.

But what they thought of it is not in the official record.


Jerusalem celebrated the UN decision with happy crowds thronging the cobbled streets and the modern thoroughfares. *Horas* sounded all night long, there was dancing and revelry. A long-held dream was coming true—the dream of generations of the dead and generations of the living. The Bible was the most read book in the city that night. Candles were lit, prayers said, thanks offered, obeisances made to the *Torah* and the prophet Abraham. The noise of *kaddish,* prayers for the dead, was drowned out in the lusty roar of a people who now felt as if they were reborn. Palestine had come alive.

Golda Meyerson and Efraim Ben-Ariel were the gayest of the *hora* dancers; they even raised their voices in song. Golda abandoned herself to the joy of the moment. So did Ariel, until he saw the familiar face in the crowd of onlookers. He motioned Golda to stop singing and dancing, his face serious now.

"Golda, stop. Stop dancing."

She laughed, whirling around. "No! This is the time to dance! Tomorrow we may not feel so much like it!"

"Stop anyway," he insisted. "Somebody wants to see you." He pointed into the crowd. She turned to see.

Morris Meyerson was standing alone, on the fringe of the crowd—a tall, stooped, more gray Morris. Golda's heart stopped. The past came back at her with a rush. "Oh, Morris. . . ." She plunged toward him, arms outstretched. Efraim Ben-Ariel remained behind. Against the background of the singing and dancing crowd they embraced gently, kissing each other on the cheek.

"Morris, dear, how are you?"

"How should I be? I'm drunk."

"You? Never."

"The whole country is drunk," Morris Meyerson said, his eyes fixing on her strangely. "With happiness. You should be the happiest one, because you worked the hardest for it. That's what I came to tell you."

"How nice of you, Morris. I appreciate it very much."

"Well, I won't keep you from your friends." He tried to withdraw but she would have none of that. Quickly she linked her arm through his.

"No, no, please. I see you so seldom any more." She drew him away from the crowd, toward the corner bus stop, watching his face fondly. He had not changed much but there was a tiredness about him, a wornness, that seemed ineradicable.

"You know, Golda, when you made your decision, I thought it was wrong. But in terms of today it was the right one."

"Thank you. I really thank you for that, Morris, because I think about my decision many times. And every day is not today," she added meaningfully. He turned to her, the old cynicism shining from his eyes again. His voice held a touch of satire.

"You mean there are days when you could possibly have doubts?"

They had reached the bus stop and Morris Meyerson halted. There was resentment and guilt in her again. They sat down on the bench by the bus stop, a sad contrast to the distant, joyful singing.

"Last Sunday, for instance," Golda murmured. "Menachem's recital."

"You knew about it? I thought, considering how busy you are, how much you travel. . . ."

"I knew. I couldn't make it."

"I'm sure Menachem understands that. I told him; everybody tells him." The sarcasm in his tone made her sit up.

"Tells him what?"

"With his mother, the country comes first."

It was as if he had stabbed her with a knife. She flashed him a bitter, chin-up smile. "You were at the recital, of course?"

"Of course."

"How did it go?"

"He plays the cello only a little bit better than Pablo Casals."

There was the old humor again. She was

delighted with that, and with his opinion. This was the Morris Meyerson she had fallen in love with as a young girl.

"Oh, Morris. I'm so glad."

"Have you heard from Sarah lately?" he asked. "I tried to phone her but that *kibbutz* is so far out in the Negev I can never get a call through. Maybe you can."

She shook her head. "I have the same trouble, so I went to see her two weeks ago."

He blinked at that. "You went all the way out there?"

"I heard from friends that Sarah wasn't feeling well. I got scared it might be the kidney problem—you know?—and I wanted to take her to Jerusalem and put her in Hadassah Hospital. But the *kibbutz* doctors were sure it was nothing serious."

"Thank God," Morris Meyerson said. Then, "You really went out there?"

"Why are you so surprised?"

"A lot of people would be surprised to know that."

Golda was hurt by the remark. "A lot of people I don't care about." He said nothing to that, but glanced down the street and then called out, "How are you, Ariel?" His tone was friendly enough.

Waiting some distance far off, but clearly visible to them both, Efraim Ben-Ariel raised his arm in a salute. Morris Meyerson looked at Golda Meyerson, the lady who still bore his name. It was a poignant moment between three people,

120

once united, now living widely different lives.

"Morris, everything's all right with you? Is there anything—"

"Everything's fine; couldn't be better. Goodby, Golda."

Morris Meyerson walked away from his wife. She let him walk. What they once had had ended years ago.

She watched him go, her face sad. Then he turned for the last time and called out, "I almost forgot the main thing I came to tell you. I heard you on the radio. You were wonderful and it was a wonderful speech."

Then he was gone, disappearing past the street light, swallowed up by the darkness. Golda Mabovitch Meyerson walked back slowly to where Efraim Ben-Ariel was waiting for her, a silent sentinel.

Yes, it had been a wonderful speech. It was fine of Morris to say so. But the Arabs could not have liked it very much.

They could hardly have thought it was wonderful, because the next day Arab attacks broke out all over Palestine. The bloodbaths had begun all over again.


The meeting of the Jewish Agency in the committee room, with David Ben-Gurion presiding, was particularly vital that hot day. Golda Meyerson, Efraim Ben-Ariel, Meged and a dozen other men, all in nondescript civilian clothes, were in attendance. It was December, and there were less than six months remaining till the date set by the United Nations for Great Britain to withdraw its forces from Palestine.

Two top military men had been summoned to give the Agency their professional appraisal of the situation: Yisrael Galili, the *Haganah* commander, and Yigael Yadin, chief of operations.

Galili was in his middle thirties; Yadin was thirty. Both men were of the alert, tense disposition that marks the military man. Galili was giving his personal overview of the Jewish chances to remain happy and whole. It was a dismal forecast all around.

"We can be sure of exactly two things: one, on May fifteenth the British will pull out. Two, on May sixteenth, the Arabs will invade."

Everybody reacted nervously to that, even Efraim Ben-Ariel, but David Ben-Gurion was calm enough, all things considered. He pushed back his shock of white hair as if to level it.

"What is the present strength of the *Haganah*?" he asked.

Yadin squared his shoulders noncommittally.

"One hundred thousand able-bodied soldiers, including women."

Efraim Ben-Ariel cut in: "And on the other side?"

Yigael Yadin said, "Four hundred thousand Arab soldiers."

Meged's eyes widened, amazed. "Four to one?"

"The regular armies of Egypt," Yadin offered grimly, "plus Syria, Lebanon, Iraq and Transjordan, if King Abdullah goes in with the Arab League."

The silence in the room held for a long time after that. Golda began writing a note on her pad. Galili spoke then. "And there is the roughest part of the problem. Abdullah's army is the Arab Legion, British trained by John Bagot Glubb and worth all the rest of their armies put together." Efraim Ben-Ariel repressed a curse. Golda passed her note to David Ben-Gurion as Galili finished his report—a most depressing one, the ultimate, dismal truth.

"If Abdullah goes in, it could be a calamity."

The Jewish Agency sat in grim silence, thinking over that bombshell.

Efraim Ben-Ariel looked at Yadin and Galili.

"Well, one way or another, what's your projection?"

Galili shrugged. "We can't make any kind of solid projection."

Ben-Gurion had scanned Golda's note but he placed it in his pocket without comment. Meged thundered, "We are asking for your professional opinion!" The request might as well have been an order.

The two military experts exchanged glances. Finally, Yigael Yadin summed up. "We might as well be honest. We say the *Haganah* has a hundred thousand soldiers. But how many are adequately trained? Ten thousand? You ask for a professional opinion, but what's my real profession? Archeology. But all right then. In my opinion we have as much of a chance to win as we have to lose."

As always, all eyes now turned to David

Ben-Gurion, the supreme leader with his white-thatched head, keen eyes and the wisdom of the ages. David Ben-Gurion smiled slowly, patiently.

"Fifty-fifty," he said flatly. "It could be worse."

Meged was shaking his head at this curious expression of optimism. Then he began to laugh, a little weakly, at the jibe. The laugh gave way to a nervous reaction which acted like a time bomb on everyone in the room. They all began to laugh uproariously.

The gallows humor of all Jews everywhere, so necessary to survival because it was a must, once again saved the day, if only temporarily.

When the meeting broke up eventually, David Ben-Gurion and Golda Meyerson walked together in the pretty garden outside the Agency building. They were entirely alone, which was good. Golda wanted desperately to talk about her scribbled memorandum.

"About your note, Golda—I didn't want to discuss it in front of the others." He sounded very thoughtful.

"Why do they think Transjordan will throw in with the Arab League?" she moaned. "King Abdullah himself assured me he wouldn't attack!"

"Our latest intelligence says the opposite," Ben-Gurion reminded her.

"I can't believe it. Let me see if Abdullah will meet me at the border again. Please."

"He won't. I made inquiries. You know our Arab expert, Ezra Danin. . . ."

"Yes, but—"

124

"Danin says that Abdullah will meet you, but not at the border. This time you would have to go to him, to his capital."

"So." Golda Meyerson nodded. "I'll go there. I'll go to Amman."

David Ben-Gurion, admiring a pretty yellow flower, turned to stare at her. "It's risky. I wouldn't let you do it, except that if somehow— God only knows how—if you could keep Abdullah out of the war, it might save us."

"When can I go?" Golda Mabovitch Meyerson asked.

David Ben-Gurion smiled. "As soon as we can get a plane." This woman—she was invincible, indomitable, the very sort of person that Israel was all about. He was amused, too, because he knew that Golda Meyerson was mortally afraid of airplanes and flying. She was not one of those angels who wanted wings.

Mrs. Golda Meir said that to her audience of children that day in Milwaukee, to their delight.

"People ask sometimes if I was nervous about flying in those little two-seater planes, especially in the days when we couldn't service them properly." How vividly she recalled the coughing engine, the fluttering flight of the Piper Cub as it ran into the air turbulence on its flight toward Amman, sinking, rolling, lurching sickeningly.

"I don't think I was very nervous. I was too worried about whether or not I'd be able to do the job I was sent to do."

She thought again of the sputtering motor, the

hissing and coughing, the young pilot adjusting the mixture of oil and gasoline as she clung to her seat for dear life. The clouds boiled and roiled all around them and the tiny aircraft; a Piper Cub was like a toy in the heavens.

"Another reason was, I could usually tell the pilot was nervous enough for both of us." And he most certainly was!

When the little plane finally set down on a desert road, with the sun blazing like a fireball, there was a car waiting for her. The man holding the door open for her in greeting was Ezra Danin, a tweedy type, scholarly looking, moustached, a vital cog in Arab-Jewish affairs. Golda knew him well and liked him, too.

"How are you, Ezra?"

"Concerned, Golda. We have a long drive to Amman, most of it in Arab territory. We will be stopped at checkpoints manned by the Arab Legion. No arrangements have been made with those soldiers. Abdullah doesn't want them to know he's receiving Jewish guests. Are you sure you should be taking such a chance?"

"Ezra Danin, it can save the life of a single Jewish soldier, I'd walk to Amman." He nodded and she entered the car. "I don't speak Arabic. What do I do about that, Danin?"

"The last thing in the world you'd think of doing, Golda Meyerson. Keep quiet."

They began the long, tortuous ride to Amman, desert outpost kingdom of Abdullah, the place where he was supreme ruler.

* * *

The barren Paletinian landscape was endless. The ride was fraught with suspense and checkpoint danger. They sped along the narrow roads, but now Golda Mabovitch Meyerson was in the traditional dark robe and veil. Ezra Danin wore the Arab *kaffiyah* headgear. Danin drove. The checkpoints, fortified outposts, began to pop up with alarming frequency.

"First checkpoint," Ezra Danin said warningly.

"What if they ask me questions?"

"A Moslem wife in the presence of her husband is not likely to be asked anything."

The checkpoint was the familiar sandbagged observation post, complete with light machine gun and armed guards. The Arab Legion ruled with an iron hand here. A corporal approached the car, gave it a long look and motioned to Danin. "Identification," he growled in Arabic. Danin accommodated him. Then the corporal gestured at Golda. "Her identification." Sitting there, uncertain, Golda did not know what to do. Danin did, however. Impatiently, he waved his ID card in her face. She made an expression of understanding, and in typical feminine fashion, made a great show of opening her handbag and fumbling into its contents. It was a clutter, of course. She started to empty the contents of the bag on the seat. The corporal grunted angrily. One of the first items that fell out was a pack of Chesterfield cigarettes. Danin went rigid at the sight of them. But he recovered very quickly, clapping a hand over the cigarettes and snarling at Golda in Arabic: "Dammit, woman, don't keep these men waiting!" The guards looked on, grinning.

Finally Golda produced her ID card. Danin snatched it from her, staying in character, and handed it to the corporal apologetically. "Damned women can drive you crazy!" Danin roared. The corporal smiled in sympathy. He looked at the ID and waved them on past the checkpoint. Ezra Danin heaved a sigh of relief. The car spurted forward, moving fast.

Danin handed her the pack of Chesterfields with a scowl.

Golda blinked. "Arab women don't smoke?"

"Not American cigarettes."

Her eyes widened in belated fright. The call was closer than even she had imagined. What a silly, stupid mistake to make!

Soon, after innumerable checkpoints, the walls of Amman loomed before them. The city wall rose like a barricade on the horizon. Golda shook herself, worn and tired as she was. Ezra Danin said, through tense lips, "We're going to the home of Abdullah's aide. The king will meet us there. He considers it safer than his palace."

Golda Mabovitch Meyerson could not have agreed more with King Abdullah. It was a wise king who knew the treachery of his subjects—an old Arabian saying.

But the Jews had one, too, a better one by far: *Love many, trust few. Always paddle your own canoe.*

She and King Abdullah had always talked the same language.

She fervently hoped she could talk to him now.

Judy Davis was very much at home in her wardrobe as young *Golda*, as she is a second-hand-store addict. Vintage clothing is her favorite way of dressing off camera.

The location for Kibbutz Merhavia was a youth village near the glide path of Ben Gurion Airport. Between the boisterous shrieks of the children and the whine of the jets, sound control was a challenge.

Leonard Nimoy, playing *Morris Meyerson, Golda's* husband, communicated in Spanish with Israelis who didn't speak English.

Judy Davis summoned up all her courage to handle a dead chicken. Being a vegetarian didn't help.

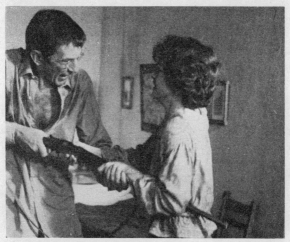

The soaring Israeli temperature (110 degrees) gave realism to Leonard Nimoy's portrayal of a man weakened by malaria.

Two of Australia's leading stars, Judy Davis and Jack Thompson, appear in the film. Prior to this picture they had never acted together.

Jack Thompson ages gracefully as he and *Golda*, now played by Ingrid Bergman, discuss concern for the country.

The baby, though a non-pro, cried in the right places. Judy Davis, aged by ten years with padding, shows the strain of poverty and motherhood.

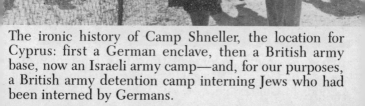

The ironic history of Camp Shneller, the location for Cyprus: first a German enclave, then a British army base, now an Israeli army camp—and, for our purposes, a British army detention camp interning Jews who had been interned by Germans.

Ingrid is superb in one of the film's most dramatic scenes, on Cyprus. Three wigs were created for different periods in Golda's life.

Ingrid's intense study of Golda's body language pays off in this suspenseful scene with *Ben Gurion*, played by English actor David de Keyser. Scene takes place at the Jewish Agency building in Jerusalem where the real Golda spent a great deal of her time. Here she says she'll go to Amman to visit *Abdullah*.

Getting a photo of the real Abdullah was a job for the researcher. Nigel Hawthorne, as *Abdullah*, practiced his Arabic for twenty-four hours. Set was former pasha's palace.

Filming the independence celebration was an extremely difficult moment for all actors, as filming took place the night of Sadat's assassination.

Golda, like Ingrid, found pleasure and relaxation in keeping house.

Ingrid's wardrobe was so authentic that many people thought the clothes belonged to the real Golda!

The white hat was supplied by a milliner who took a polaroid picture of Bergman wearing it, as a memento, then later got the hat back.

*Golda* embraces a soldier at the Wall at the end of the Six-Day War, a re-enactment of the world-famous photo.

*Lou Kaddar* and *Golda*. Anne Jackson, who portrays *Lou* became a good friend of the real Lou Kaddar, Golda's secretary.

This photo, depicting *Golda* and her staff in a strategy conference, appeared in the Israeli press, marking observance of the Yom Kippur War (1973).

*Golda* and *Moshe Dayan*, played by Yossi Graber. The real Dayan kindly validated the historical accuracy of the script.

*Golda* and *Sadat* (Robert Loggia). For the first time it is revealed that Golda gave Sadat a gold locket for his new granddaughter. Robert Loggia spent over three hours being made up to achieve the effect. The producers felt homage should be paid to Sadat, and Loggia's role was expanded.

Judy Davis had lunch alone with Ingrid Bergman for their first meeting. She confided she was extremely nervous but was soon put at ease by Ingrid.

It was never difficult to find the director, Alan Gibson, as his 6'6" frame was easily spotted.

The life of Golda Meir is the history of a nation. A great actress plays a great lady.

And make him understand. What the Jews of Palestine needed.

"*Shalom,*" Golda Mabovitch Meyerson said, in the living room of the aide to King Abdullah. Middle Eastern adornments and trappings were all about; the floors were polished and the furnishings were oriental antiques. King Abdullah came forward to greet her, smiling, affable, warmhearted. "*Salaam,* Madame. *Salaam,* Danin, my friend." His words were Arabic but Golda knew their meaning. Ezra Danin bowed. "*Wa aleykum as-salaam,* Your Majesty."

Everyone sat down, except the bodyguards stationed at either end of the room. King Abdullah helped himself to a cigarette from an ivory inlaid box on the mosaic coffee table. He offered Golda one. She took it and he lighted it for her. "Thank you," she said, simply. Abdullah's eyes roved over her, approving of the Moslem garb. In keeping with his regal title, he wore traditional Arab robes. His dusky face, though moustached, bearded and strong, was oddly angelic. When he spoke it was in a sweet, calm voice. But it was a powerful voice all the same. Golda knew him well, knew he was a lordly Arab.

"And what else may I do for you, Mrs. Meyerson?"

"I've already said in one word what I came here for: *Shalom.* Peace—that's what we all want."

"Peace is all I want."

"Your Majesty, the last time you and I met, we talked about what you believed to be the role of

145

the Jews in the scheme of things."

"Yes," Abdullah recalled, with a gentle smile on his face. "I believed with all my heart that God had scattered the Jews throughout the Western world for a purpose. His divine purpose was for you to absorb Western knowledge and progress and then return to the Middle East and share it with us, your fellow Semites."

Golda nodded. He had remembered, to the word. "You told me that you would always be our friend, that you would never join in any attack against us."

"I am still your friend."

"But a few months ago we heard that you were under pressure to join with those who intend to attack us."

"I am always under pressure."

"I sent you a note. I've never forgotten your answer. You said, 'Madame, I am a Bedouin, and a Bedouin always keeps his word. I am also a king, and a king must keep his word. Beyond all that, I never break a promise I give to a woman.'" She paused deliberately to let that sink it. "What is the status of that promise now?"

King Abdullah's reaction was not what she had expected, surely not what she had bargained for. The dark face mottled with anger, the body trembled, and Abdullah whirled in the direction of Ezra Danin, in an abrupt flareup of monumental anger. He boomed, "Why do you people send me a woman to deal with me? It is insulting! The Jews traditionally have not held women in much greater esteem than Moslems have!"

Danin tried to keep the peace. "Your Majesty, she is the head of our political action department," he said, diplomatically.

"Why do you give such an important position to a woman?"

Danin said softly, "Perhaps this is a part of the progress which, as Your Majesty believes, we were scattered throughout the Western world to absorb." He smiled. "*Inshallah,* the will of God."

"*Inshallah,*" King Abdullah echoed. "I suppose I'll have to accept that." He turned back to Golda Meyerson. "My dear madame, when I made that promise, I was alone. Now I am one of five. I cannot make decisions alone any more."

Masking her feelings at this great betrayal, this vast disappointment, Golda kept her voice calm and steady. This was no place or time for tears. She still had a job to do, *the* job. So she appealed to logic.

"It might pay you to keep your independence. As long as there's peace, we will honor the borders set by the United Nations, including international control of Jerusalem. We've accepted all that. But if we're attacked and we have to fight, that's all off. We'll take whatever territory we can to improve our position."

King Abdullah was not impressed.

"With five countries against you, I don't see how you can take much territory."

"You don't know how our strength has increased in the last months."

She glanced sidelong at Ezra Danin. Perhaps it was no lie and Abdullah didn't know. Danin kept his scholar's face bland, and waited. King Abdullah was regarding Golda with a strange interest now.

"I understand you have a daughter who lives on a *kibbutz* in the Negev. Revivim."

With some surprise, Golda could only answer, "Yes."

"I happen to know it is directly in the path of the Egyptian army's plan of attack. You should take your daughter away to someplace safe."

Golda Meyerson checked her impulse to panic. "I appreciate your telling me this, I really do, but most of the other young people at Revivim have mothers, too. And if all the mothers take their children away, who will stop the Egyptians?"

"I accept that." Abdullah nodded slowly. "Your children will do their duty, and I will do mine. And the result will be a lot of bloodshed and destruction—which would have been very easy to avoid."

"Just tell me how," Golda pleaded.

"Don't proclaim your state," he said, sternly. "Not now. Why are you in such a hurry?"

"We've been waiting two thousand years. I wouldn't call that being in a hurry, Your Majesty."

His smile was warmer, friendlier. "I accept that too. But why can't you wait a few more years? Here is my offer. I will take over all of Palestine. The Jews may continue to live there under my protection. You will be represented in my parliament. I will treat you very well."

Golda did not answer. Danin was silent, too.

"You have my promise," Abdullah intoned. "Don't you believe it?"

"Promises are not good enough for us any more."

"That is the only way I can help you!" The fury rose in Abdullah's voice again. His face worked. "Why are you so stubborn as to refuse me?"

"Because we must have our own state, and the time is now!" Her voice rose to match his. "And if the only way we can have it is to go to war, then we'll go to war!" She stared squarely at him. "And we will beat you!"

That was too much for King Abdullah. He leaped to his feet, and strode up and down, gesturing furiously. He waved his arms in a tirade, a torrent of anger at this woman who challenged him in his own domain. A mere *woman!*

"I will not put up with her insults! I have had enough!" That was shouted in Arabic, but Golda understood his meaning, anyway. "If there is a war," he continued in English, "it will be her fault, all her fault, because she is a stubborn, arrogant, damned *woman!*"

Ezra Danin moved to Golda protectively, afraid of what King Abdullah might do in his outrage. Around them, the Arab bodyguards had never looked more dangerous. Their expressions were menacing, for they were not blind to their lord and ruler's rage or the cause of it— Golda Mabovitch Meyerson, the Jewish female.

Nevertheless, Golda shook off Danin and walked deliberately and coolly toward King

Abdullah. He almost retreated before her.

"Your Majesty, let's suppose it was a mistake to send me here. Would it be helpful for you to meet David Ben-Gurion?"

The suggestion seemed to calm him. He thought briefly, pacified a little, and then candidly admitted, "Not really. If Mr. Ben-Gurion were to announce that he had made peace with me, he would be hailed as a hero. If I announced that I had made peace with him, I would be murdered."

That was the bottom line, the entire ball of wax. There was no more to be said, no more to be done. Golda Mabovitch Meyerson looked at King Abdullah. It was over. Less than four years after this meeting Abdullah would be shot dead by an Arab assassin. It was a murder of political expedience.

At that time she had thought: Dear God, what would have happened to us had we been a minority in an Arab country, under his protection! She knew the answer all too well.

There was nothing left to do that night but for her and Ezra Danin to retire in defeat from King Abdullah's presence. Shaken and very morose, they returned to their car. The thing dominant in Golda's mind was that the Arab Legion was joining four other armies against the Jews, and the Legion had tanks.

The Jews had nothing but great trouble on their horizon once more, as always. So it had been since the dawn of Mankind.

All through the long and dangerous trip back from Amman to Palestine, Golda Mabovitch

Meyerson could only think of one thing. It haunted her every mile of the journey.

She said to herself: *I failed. There will be war.* And so she had. And so there was.

# BOOK TWO

## Israel

"If not now, when?"

—Hillel, Hebrew sage

# *Memories*

---

The fascinated children in the auditorium could not take their eyes from the elderly woman seated on the platform before them. The story Mrs. Golda Meir was telling them had everything that all the great stories had. It was like *Alice in Wonderland, Treasure Island, The Wizard of Oz;* the big difference was, this was a true story. All this had really happened once, before any of them were born. It was something to think about.

Milwaukee, in 1977, suddenly seemed like a pretty nice place to be alive in, grow up in, go to school in.

"I don't suppose any of you children have ever talked a lot braver than you felt," the golden old woman said, and everybody laughed at that in wry appreciation.

"Well then you can understand how frightened I was, no matter what I said to King Abdullah. His army had tanks. And there was only four months to go before the British left."

The years rolled back again, the mists of memory parted for all to see, and suddenly they were in Jerusalem again, in the year 1948. "When I reported to Ben-Gurion, he was with the leaders of the Jewish Agency, listening to our treasurer, who had just returned from America. He was a man named Eliezer Kaplan—a middle-aged man, a worrier, a businessman. I arrived for the meeting by car—getting there late, I must admit. I took my seat quietly and Mr. Ben-Gurion looked at me the way Mr. Macy might when you come late for class. Mr. Kaplan was already making his full report to the Agency."

It was to be very important, this meeting. The Jewish Agency had to face realities.

The Jews of Palestine needed money always but there was not much to be had any more—not from America, at any rate, according to Eliezer Kaplan, Treasurer.

"I got the strong impression," Kaplan reported in his nasal voice, "that the American Jewish community is tired of supporting us. We have made so many urgent appeals to them for money that they're not listening any more. I think we have to face reality, as bitter as it is. We cannot count on anything over five million dollars from America."

Eliezer Kaplan terminated his report and everyone around the conference table looked at David Ben-Gurion, that distiller of all news. He was the barometer of the Agency. What did he think of this? Golda stared at the Great Man, too, as anxious as anyone else to know.

David Ben-Gurion pyramided his fingers and said matter-of-factly, "We have bought and paid for ten thousand rifles, two hundred light machine guns, two-point-five million cartridges. That is fine for fighting infantry, but against artillery, tanks and airplanes, we might as well throw stones." He sighed deeply. "We must come as close as possible to the equipment of a modern army. We must have some planes of our own; heavy machine guns, mortars and flame throwers; and tons of steel to armor plate cars and trucks until we can get some tanks."

Kaplan coughed apologetically. "B-G, you know you can't equip this modern army of yours for five million dollars."

"Correct. We must have twenty-five million, at least."

"Where are we going to get it?" Kaplan demanded unhappily.

David Ben-Gurion smiled grimly. "There's only one place in the world where we can raise so much money in so little time. I'm going to the United States immediately. I will make our American friends understand how serious the situation is."

Golda Mabovitch Meyerson interrupted. "Excuse me, B-G, but you can't possibly leave at a time like this." Before he could answer that she had rushed on. "Look, what you're doing here I can't do. But I might be able to do what you want to do in America." This clearly miffed David Ben-Gurion and he scowled at her darkly. His tone was sarcastic when he replied to her suggestion.

"What makes you think you can raise that kind of money?"

"Two things. I speak the language. . . ."

"So do I," he cut in tersely. "What's the other?"

She smiled. "I'm an American."

"No," he barked, his face falling. "This is too important."

"Let's put it to a vote," Golda said quickly.

"A vote!" He was horrified. A gasp ran around the table. "Are you calling for a vote to overrule me?"

"Why not?" Meged, smiling, broke in happily. "We are founding the only democracy in the Middle East. In a democracy the majority rules. Those in favor of sending Golda. . . ."

There was a sudden affirmative chorus of *Ayes* from all around the room. David Ben-Gurion paled a little.

"Opposed?" Meged continued, looking around. No hands or nays. "None. Golda goes." All the men smiled and looked at David Ben-Gurion to see how he would take this defeat in his own backyard.

"Nu," David Ben-Gurion rumbled. "Democracy!"

Which was how Golda Mabovitch Meyerson got to go to the United States of America to raise twenty-five million dollars, an idea that had been her very own in the first place.

In her Tel Aviv apartment, Golda Meyerson packed for her trip to America. Hastily, for she was eager to be gone. She did not intend to take much more than one suitcase and the clothes on her back. Efraim Ben-Ariel had come to see her off. From his position on the couch, he was regarding her with a mixture of love and admiration as she hurried back and forth between suitcase and closet and the drawers of the bureau.

"Do you have a proper coat? It's cold in New York."

"I don't have any coat. I'll buy one there."

"Wouldn't it be better to leave a day later and buy one here?"

"Probably. But Ben-Gurion insists I take the plane this afternoon. Does one argue with B-G?"

"Why?"

"Ha. I think he's getting even with me for this morning."

Ariel smiled, but then he said soberly, "What a life. We don't even have time for each other, let alone ourselves." His tone was wistful.

Golda looked at him fondly. "My Ariel, maybe when I get back from America—"

"I probably won't be here."

"Really? Where are you going?"

"Pilsen," he said flatly.

"Pilsen," she echoed. "What's there?"

"They make a great beer in Pilsen. Pilsener beer is famous."

Golda Mabovitch Meyerson snapped her suitcase shut and stared at him concernedly. "Ariel, what is this? You're not going to Czechoslovakia to drink beer."

He was so silent at that, she went to the couch to sit down beside him. "I have to leave right away, Ariel. Please tell me."

She put her warm hand softly on his. Efraim Ben-Ariel looked at her deeply. "You know we've been trying to put together some kind of air force for the *Haganah*." She nodded and he went on. "Ehud's made a deal to buy Messerschmitt 109 fighter planes. You can't imagine what an assortment of pilots we have standing by: U.S. Air Corps and RAF veterans, Jews and non-Jews—God bless them. But none of this is worth a damn without mechanics to service the planes."

"Yes. Go on."

"What's in Pilsen besides beer is the Skoda Munitions Works, which turned out Messerschmitts for the Germans. I'm going there to hire aircraft mechanics."

She thought that over, frowning. "Well, of course I know the Czech government has been selling us arms. But the situation is very unstable there now."

At his nod, she continued. "By the time you get there the Soviet Union could be running things—and I wouldn't trust that bunch of bums to be any friends of ours. How do you know they'd let a Jewish agent into the country?"

Ariel admitted he didn't know. "I don't. And I don't have time to be held up at the border while they bury me in red tape."

"So?" She eyed him suspiciously. "Do you have some answer for that?"

His smile was fleeting, casual. "It's dark at

night. Barbed wire can be cut."

"And sentries? What do you do about sentries?"

"Deal with them," he replied curtly. "One way or another."

Her distress with his mission was all too apparent in her face. She rose to her feet and began to pace the room. Her strides were nervous, high strung. She whirled on him suddenly, crying out in anguish.

"No. Don't do it, Ariel, please. Give up the whole idea. It's wrong for you."

"Why is it wrong for me?"

"Because—you're badly needed here. Let somebody else go."

He had stiffened at her words. "I'm one of the very few who speak the language, Golda."

"But there are others!" she shouted, helpless to keep her voice from rising. "For hiring mechanics, any businessman would be better!"

He shook his head, his eyes proud. "How many businessmen do we have with commando training?"

"Training is one thing! This is different!"

"What's different about it?" he asked calmly.

"You're too old!" she wailed, miserable and frightened.

Efraim Ben-Ariel came to her then, smiling his gentle smile and putting his arms about her. The tall, lithe body was still muscular but there was gray in the dark hair, a line or two in the strong face that had not been there a few years ago.

"Am I too old for you, Golda?" he asked softly.

"For me—oh, no," she murmured, tearfully. "For me you're a long way from it."

"Then what am I old for?"

"For being caught, being sent to a Soviet prison camp. We're both too old for that. We'd never see each other again."

He caught her fast in his arms, staring into her troubled eyes. "Golda, I love it that you feel this way. But do you really think you can talk me out of going?"

"Not for a minute," Golda Mabovitch Meyerson said, with great pride in him and what he was in her voice and eyes. He was the same kind of Jew she was. With them Palestine came first, the Cause came first.

They locked in a long, ardent embrace the more earnest and loving because it could very well be their last one. Finally she pushed away from him with deep regret. "I have to leave," she whispered. "I have to leave right now."

Efraim Ben-Ariel's expression was a study in irony.

"I know. What a life—not even time to say goodby."

They were not to meet again for a long, long time, but neither of them knew that then—not for sure, anyway.

Chicago, Illinois, U.S.A., was a nightmare of automobiles, taxis and people wherever the eye could see, a vast difference from Palestine with its desert and wastelands. It was cold in America, too, with chill, biting winds. Golda Meyerson had come to Chicago straight from New York because there happened to be an important convention in Chicago. The Council of the Jewish Federations was meeting there. In her new coat, Golda rushed by taxi to the convention hall, in the company of a public relations man named Stampler. Stampler was bright eyed and bushy tailed, but just a shade too negative about Golda's chances with the council heads and their people. Either that, or he had had experiences that made him wary.

"You have to understand, Mrs. Meyerson," Stampler explained as the cab whisked through the crowded city streets, "this is not a Zionist organization. Some of these people—maybe a lot of them—are just not interested in Palestine."

"And all of them are sick and tired," Golda agreed, "of hearing how badly we need money. Right, Mr. Stampler?"

He was pleased that she understood the situation.

"Besides, frankly, they're under pressure to raise funds for institutions in America—Jewish hospitals and other Jewish charities all over the country. They need money, too."

Stampler, getting no response from the calm woman looking out the cab windows at Chicago's stone face, rushed on. "It might be better if you didn't address the group, Mrs. Meyerson. Wait and let me set up a more favorable audience."

"No. I have to try and get through to these people."

"Well, then, it might be a good idea to let me

look over your speech. I could give you a few pointers."

"I haven't prepared a speech," she said simply.

Stampler was shocked. "You don't know what you're going to say?"

"I'll know," Golda Mabovitch Meyerson said placidly but determinedly, "when the time comes."

The cab continued toward the convention hall. Mr. Stampler collapsed against the cushions, defeated. He had never met or known a woman like this before.

The audience in the convention hall was as indifferent and, perhaps, hostile as Stampler had said they would be. Looking out at a sea of more than two hundred well-dressed men and women, Mrs. Golda Meyerson saw she was clearly a controversial speaker. A mild murmur of unrest was traveling through the crowd as she spoke. But the woman who had lived in Palestine during the early days of struggle, and had known privation and worse, was not dismayed. She chose her words carefully and sent them out to her audience with quiet authority and sincerity.

"Please believe me when I tell you that I have not come to the United States only because several hundred thousand Jews are in danger of being killed. That is not the issue."

On the podium where she alone stood, several dignitaries were seated behind her, trying to look interested, not bored.

Golda raised her voice a little, building in vocal

164

power. "The issue is that if the Jews of Palestine survive, then the Jews of the world survive with them and their freedom will be assured forever. But if these several hundred thousand are wiped off the face of the earth, then there will be no Jewish people as such—and for centuries to come, all our hopes and dreams of a Jewish nation, a Jewish homeland, will be smashed."

Silence reigned in the great hall. The audience was remarkably quiet now. "My friends, when I say we need money immediately, I don't mean next week—I mean right now. In less than four months we will be fighting for our lives against cannon and armor."

Again no response. No sound. No murmurs of anything. "It is not for you to decide whether we will fight. That decision is taken: we will fight. We will pay for the birth of our nation with our blood. That is normal. The best among us will fall. That is certain. You can decide only one thing!" Mrs. Golda Meyerson challenged them all with her eyes and her next words. "Whether we win or we lose."

That was the last of what she had to say.

She turned from the microphone and stared out stiffly at the faces before her. Nobody stirred; there was not a sound. And then it started—a ripple of applause, then a rising tide of approbation that turned into a torrent of acclaim, agreement and affection. Golda Mabotvitch Meyerson blinked in wonder. People were on their feet, shouting, calling out words. And behind her, on the podium, all the dignitaries were now standing, applauding wildly.

Tears of gratitude stained the cheeks of Golda Meyerson.

Whatever she had said, whatever she had done, she had won—here in Chicago, at least. There were Jews in America who still cared what was going on in Palestine and were still willing to do something about it. Mr. Stampler began to think of her as a spellbinder, a witch, a great orator, someone very special as a speaker. For once he was correct.

Golda Meyerson's tour to raise funds for Palestine took her to Jewish communities all over the United States. Whenever and wherever she spoke, American Jews listened, understood, wept, and opened their checkbooks, dug into their treasuries. Money poured into the Jewish Cause.

The results were incredible—so much so that, months later, David Ben-Gurion telephoned her all the way from Palestine, catching her in one of the countless hotel rooms she had lived in during her tour of the United States. He had to raise his voice over the transatlantic wire, but it was worth it. Palestine was rejoicing in the accomplishments of its Agent Extraordinaire to America.

"Golda, from the reports I hear you're doing wonders! Tell me, so far have you gotten twenty-five million dollars?"

She was sitting up in bed to answer the phone; she had been sleeping when the call came. "No,

B-G," she said sleepily.

"You didn't?" His voice was surprised.

She smiled at his tone, a little human smile of justifiable pride in herself. "So far I got us fifty."

Far off in distant Palestine, David Ben-Gurion clutched the phone in his fingers in an amalgam of excitement, joy and amazement. His keen eyes brimmed with happiness. With women like Golda on their side, how could the Jews lose?

And then came the Day of Days, the one that Jews had waited for since the dawn of time.

On May 14, 1948, David Ben-Gurion, flanked by every official in the Jewish Agency, every important person in the goverment of Palestine, stood on the steps of the Tel Aviv Museum. It was a bright, sun-filled day and the Lord was in his heaven, indeed. Some two hundred people had gathered in the open air to hear what Ben-Gurion had to say to mark, to signify, to commemorate this greatest of all days in Palestine.

The white-thatched head shone in the sunlight. The words rang out like silver bells, each one sharp and clear. ". . . exiled from the land of Israel . . . the Jewish people have returned . . . believing in their self-evident right to be a nation, like all other nations, in their own sovereign state. . . ."

There was not a dry eye out there before him, not a heart that did not beat a little faster. Even the children were hushed.

"By virtue of this right, and the Resolution of the General Assembly of the United Nations, we

167

hereby proclaim the establishment of the Jewish State in Palestine, to be called Israel."

No one answered that. No one spoke, cheered or shouted.

Then, suddenly, a few of the people before him began to sing, and soon they were all singing as one, proudly, happily, feelingly, the song that made them a people. The words of *Hatikvoh* filled the air. The Jews had their National Anthem already.

David Ben-Gurion, the man who was to be Israel's first Premier, sang along with everyone else.

Golda Meyerson had known all along that any people who declare their independence must go through great difficulties. But for herself, and the Jewish people, despite the deadly dangers that independence would entail, it was worth it. They were determined to do it anyway—to be *free*.

Another hotel room in America. Another phone call from David Ben-Gurion. A weary Golda Meyerson answered the summons, to hear Ben-Gurion's familiar voice barking over the long distance line.

"Golda! I've been trying to reach you. Where've you been?"

"Where?" She laughed. "At a meeting. Don't ask which one; I can hardly think which city I'm in any more."

"Then you don't know what's happened?"

Fear clutched at her heart for a moment, waking her from lethargy. "No. What happened?

What?"

"President Truman has recognized Israel!" David Ben-Gurion proclaimed jubilantly. It was another great moment, to be recognized by the President of the United States—feisty, plain-talking, bluntly honest Truman. A tiny sob escaped from Golda Meyerson. She was overcome with emotion, stunned.

"Golda?" Ben-Gurion was amazed. "Are you crying? Why are you crying *now*?"

Golda with tearful pride, said clearly, "I'm an American, remember?"

And so she was. But she was also a Jew, and Israel was her home. The Israel that had been Palestine. The Holy Land.

That night, Egyptian Spitfires bombed Tel Aviv, swooping down from the dark skies to strafe, bombard and pummel the city. It was the Arab answer to President Truman's gesture, the back-of-the-hand reply.

The next day, May fifteenth, right on schedule, Israel was invaded by the armies of five countries: Egypt, Syria, Lebanon, Jordan and Iraq. Additional troops were contributed to the assault by Saudi Arabia. The Jews were not going to be allowed to enjoy their new statehood; King Abdullah had called the shot back there in Amman.

There was cannon fire; shells exploding all over the countryside; the air filled with the unforgettable sounds of violence and sudden death.

In the Jordan Valley, where Syria had begun attacking even before the British pullout from

169

Palestine, several *kibbutzim* faced total annihilation. The Arabs would not be merciful.

And where was Golda Mabovitch Meyerson fighting the War of Independence? In America.

Mr. Stampler simply could not understand Mrs. Meyerson's preoccupation with the events in war-torn Israel while he briefed her on her busy speaker's schedule. She just wouldn't get her shapely nose out of the daily newspapers; she read them all the time, looking concerned and worried. Stampler lost his temper once, in a cab ride to one more function.

Golda smiled at him charitably. "You public relations people will have to be very patient with me, Mr. Stampler. My mind is much on the war news—which is unbearable to me, as you must know."

"Sorry, Mrs. Meyerson."

"Don't be sorry for me. Be sorry for the Jews of Israel."

It reached a point when even he could see how horrible the war news must be for Mrs. Golda Meyerson. The details were right there, every day, in American papers.

Out of one hundred and fifty people in one *kibbutz* overrun by Arab hordes there were exactly four survivors. The Arab legion had cut off the Old City of Jerusalem and was savagely shelling the Jewish Quarter. The *Haganah* tried to come from the New City but failed. The corpses mounted higher and higher every day. Finally, the Jewish Quarter surrendered. There were thirteen hundred survivors, mostly women, children and old *rabbis.*

No, the newspapers could not be fun reading for Golda Meyerson, but Stampler had his own job to do—which he did very well. "Mrs. Meyerson? Let me run through this again. We go from here to Denver and from Denver to Los Angeles."

But she was reading aloud from the newspaper held in her hands. "Six thousand soldiers killed—one percent of our population." She turned grimly to Stampler. "Do you know what that would be in terms of the United States population?"

"Well, ah—" Stampler was trapped. "No, I don't."

"That would be one and a half million killed, Mr. Stampler."

His reaction was genuine. "Good God!"

Golda read from the newspaper again. "A reliable source says that in another seventy-two hours it will be all over."

She looked at Stampler. He was gravely silent, which was remarkable for young Mr. Stampler.

She turned to stare bleakly out the taxi window.

Neither of them could have foreseen that Golda Meyerson's fund-raising tour across the United States would grow very large and important in the next three days.

Before those crucial seventy-two hours had expired, vital weapons, bought with the donated monies which Golda Meyerson had won, began to arrive in chartered ships. Freighters bobbed in the port waters of Palestine, unloading their cargoes of crates and equipment for war—rifles, hand grenades, artillery pieces. One of the first ships from Pilsen brought ten Messerschmitt fighter planes, and aircraft mechanics from Czechoslovakia. Then the tide began to turn for the new state of Israel.

Now, the Israeli infantry advanced. Israeli artillery fired back at its Arab enemies. The World War II fighter planes now bore Israeli markings. They came down out of the blue skies to hammer the Arab Legion, to machine gun Arabs and blow up Arab installations. Israeli soldiers now walked through captured Arab villages.

In a few more days, the Arabs were being driven back, or at least contained on all fronts. And the world wondered and marveled at this days-old nation which was fighting brilliantly for its survival. There was still blood, slaughter, and calamity, but Israel was holding its own—for the time being, at least. Courage, determination, military skill against overwhelming odds were taking on new meanings. These Israelis were titans in combat. They knew how to fight, and perhaps to win.

With her great work in America done, Golda Mabovitch Meyerson was allowed to return home to Israel—the new land, the new homeland. Golda had no notion of what would be awaiting her when her plane touched down at Lydda Airport.

It was to be Hail the Conquering Hero, but she did not know that as her airliner winged its way across the Atlantic, racing the sun. She had never lost her basic humility. She never would, for all of her vast accomplishments. That was something even young Stampler had found out about her, from the very beginning of their association. She had left America with his heart and admiration in her pocket. There was only one Golda Meyerson.

When the airliner door opened, after the DC-6's wheels were anchored unmovingly on the Lydda Airport strip, Golda Mabovitch Meyerson stepped through. The sun was in her eyes; it was another hot Israeli day. But she was able to see, and stop in amazement and wonder at the spectacle before her—the reception committee which had come to welcome her home. There was David Ben-Gurion, white haired, smiling, with every other official from the Agency flanking him, all of them waving and shouting. Then a car pulled up and a tall man in uniform alighted—a very familiar man, Efraim Ben-Ariel! Golda hurried down the plane steps. Ariel hurried to meet her, running. Ben-Gurion and the others stood back and watched, knowing, as everyone knew, how they felt.

Through a mist of tears, Golda and Ariel touched hands, then kissed each other on the cheek in the European style. It seemed casual, but their hands held in a long, fervent clasp. Ben-Gurion and the officials surged forward then, all talking at once, reaching for Golda. Ariel moved back to permit them to talk with her.

David Ben-Gurion's expression was grave but his words were warmer than a fire in a *kibbutz* on a cold desert night. "*Shalom,* Golda. I'm going to make you a speech—but very short, so don't expect much."

She laughed happily. "All right, B-G."

"One day, when history is written, it will record that there was a woman who made it possible for the Jewish State to be born."

It was a great moment, again, a lifetime crowded into one heartfelt eulogy. Golda was overcome. She could only look into David Ben-Gurion's keen eyes, as he was looking at her. They eyed each other with warm, deep appreciation and gratitude, for having worked together in this twisted, cruel, unhappy yet so joyous life, this Jewish life.

"*Shalom,* B-G," she said.

"*Shalom,* Golda," he replied.

Efraim Ben-Ariel, standing back watching, brushed at his own eyes. It was a great moment, for him, too, who had known her since Merhavia.

Israel's First Lady—and who better deserved such a title—had come home again. The prodigal daughter had returned in triumph, glory and love. Israel would not die, could not die, with women like this in its ranks. Damn the Arabs. Damn tyrants. Damn dictators. Israel would survive!

The warm sun, the bright airfield, the blue sky, the fleecy white clouds: it was all perfect, as if God himself had arranged this homecoming for this very special woman. Golda Mabovitch Meyerson was glad to be home. It was where she belonged, nowhere else. It was life to her, the Good Life as promised in the Old Testament.

# *Equality*

---

The General Assembly of the United Nations had its hands full in those early days of war and confusion. The whole world was watching, waiting to see what it would do about the Arabs and Israel. It was a tense, trying time for everyone.

When the Arab countries in the United Nations General Assembly accepted a proposal for a cease fire—for the fighting had become a bloody reversal for them—Israel was left with some gains over the partition plan, but with the Old City still in Jordanian hands. Still, the UN decision was something. Israel had gained breathing space, time in which to rebuild the havoc and destruction of the early days of the war.

For Zionists it was a victory, all things considered. They had held five Arabian countries in check, kept them from wiping out the people of the Star of David.

The price had been high but the outcome was sweet.

There was a chance for Israel now—hope, that

ephemeral thing that always sprang eternal within the human breast. In the Jewish breast, hope was a concrete reality now.

Israel had won a reprieve from destruction and obliteration. The Star of David would continue to fly on all flags over Israel. The Arab invaders would have to put up with it, even if they never would stop fighting.

For the next nineteen years, Jews were not permitted to visit their holiest site, the Western Wall of the Temple. This was in direct violation of the United Nations resolution calling for free access to all holy places. No place was holier to the Jews than the great Wailing Wall in East Jerusalem, built with the stones from Herod's Temple, where the Jews had come to worship since Biblical times. This was cruel, denying religious Jews what they needed most: spiritual comfort and guidance. The Arab Christians of Israel were permitted visits to their holy shrines and places only at Christmas and Eastertime.

With all this, the problem of the Palestinian refugees was created. And Golda Meyerson, along with every other conscientious Jew, lived through all these wretched years wondering when all the madness would end—if it would actually end in her lifetime.

She was certain in her mind and heart that some Palestinian Arabs fled because they were frightened. But she also knew that many left because their leaders told them to, promising that after the Jews were driven into the sea they could return and take over Jewish property. Of course the Jews refused to be driven into the sea, so these refugees became homeless. None of the Arab countries would give them a home. Only two countries would even let them in, and those confined them all to refugee camps. These would prove to be the only people in history to remain refugees after thirty years. But Israel, merciful always, took in hundreds of thousands of Jewish refugees from the Arab countries. Whether they spoke Hebrew or Arabic, it mattered not; a Jew was a Jew was a Jew, always.

David Ben-Gurion became the first Prime Minister of Israel. He appointed Golda Mabovitch Meyerson to his cabinet as Minister of Labor. And he initiated the suggestion that Golda Meyerson should have an assistant to help her with her onerous duties. A lucky stroke, a happy thought, because it brought a lady named Lou Kaddar into Golda Meyerson's life—a lady who was to prove indispensable, and a great friend all the way up to Milwaukee, 1977, and thereafter until the bitter end, when the Golda Meir story reached its ultimate conclusion.

But that day in Golda's Tel Aviv office, Lou Kaddar, selling herself just a little, but too proud to beg, made her first entrance into the life of Golda Meyerson. With the office desk between them the ladies measured each other. It was the first meeting of two very special women.

"I speak English. French even better," Lou Kaddar said in a vibrant, clear, confident voice. "I was born in France."

Golda studied the handsome woman seated across from her, liking instantly the clean, chiseled face, the erect head and posture, the firm speaking voice.

She smiled. "How are you at writing letters?"

"Would you like to see a sample?"

Golda took the paper Lou extracted from her bag and handed across the desk. She smiled. "I read that an old stevedoring company executive has just died. You might care to send a letter of condolence."

Golda read for a moment, marveling at the felicitous prose. "What a beautiful letter! Did you know this man?"

"Actually, yes."

"Was he as much of a saint as you make out here?"

"He was a son of a bitch," Lou Kaddar said succinctly.

"You might be very good for this job," Golda said. "Do you think you would like working for me?"

"I would love it," Lou Kaddar said without hesitation.

"How do you know you'd love it?"

"I was in the *Haganah*. I was wounded and I haven't worked since I got out of the hospital. Madame Minister, I'm tired of being hungry all the time."

Golda nodded, impressed. She could always understand motivation like that. "That's a good answer. All right. As far as I'm concerned the job is yours."

180

Lou Kaddar smiled her appreciation.

"But I'll have to check with Ben-Gurion before I make it definite."

"Oh. Will that be a problem?" A note of fear edged into the tone.

"Absolutely not. No problem at all," Golda said firmly.

In David Ben-Gurion's office later that day, Golda Meyerson proposed the name of her new assistant. The Prime Minister shuffled papers on his desk and growled disapprovingly.

"What's her name again?"

"Kaddar. Lou Kaddar."

"Never heard of her."

Golda, standing, already worried, pushed on. "B-G, the point is not whether you ever heard of her. . . ."

"Correct. The point is, you don't need her. I'm sending you a very fine man. He's been liasion to the Zionist office in Geneva. He can write you effective speeches not only in Hebrew but in English, French and Spanish. Plus he's a great administrator. He'll make your staff run like a watch. His name is Rothenburg."

"Well," Golda Meyerson said, "you certainly seem impressed with him. Enthusiastic, I might say."

"I am very enthusiastic," Ben-Gurion said.

"Fine. You take Rothenburg for your assistant. I'll take Lou Kaddar for mine."

Before he could look up from his clutter of papers, startled at her defiance, she had left the office, slamming the door slightly as she left. The gesture was pure rebellion. Same old Golda Meyerson, David Ben-Gurion reflected rue-fully—still doing all things as she saw fit to do them.

Israel had peace now, or what was hoped would be peace. And with it came a tidal wave of immigrants: Jews not only from Europe, but from Libya, Tunisia, Morocco, Afghanistan, India, Yemen. The Minister of Labor had to find all these people jobs or they would become mill-stones about the neck of the new country. So Golda Meyerson did find some of them jobs, as many of them as she could. Construction of one-story buildings was a project, with donkeys still in use to help with the work. It might be make-shift but it was honest work for willing hands. Golda set the wheels of industry and labor in motion, and in her role as minister oversaw all that went on. Indeed, she made a habit of visiting the work sites to see how things were going and what the mood of the laborers was.

One such time was the day she visited Herman Friedenthal, the supervisor of one of these build-ing projects. Golda found him surrounded by a dozen men in native garb, mixing and hauling cement. Friedenthal was the only one wearing conventional work clothes, overalls and heavy shoes. He also had an air of fatherliness.

"*Shalom*, Mr. Friedenthal! How is it going?"

He smiled in greeting but his tone was trou-bled. "Well, Madame Minister, you have to un-derstand that these men have never held a brick or a cement block in their hands before."

"I do, of course. We rely on you to teach them."

"Oh, they learn quickly. But I have a problem."

"Yes?"

"In my group there are ten men. And I only speak six languages."

The Minister of Labor had her heartiest laugh in months.

And the work went on. The jobs went on.

The Yemenites, for instance, did not know what beds were for. They slept *under* them, for protection of some nebulous kind. Their ignorance of flush toilets was beyond discussion. But before long they were in apartments—and complaining there wasn't enough hot water. That was progress, to Golda Mabovitch Meyerson.

Work never hurt anyone. Everyone *needed* to work. It was God's will, his method of keeping people alive for something better than they already had.

Lou Kaddar observed Golda Meyerson very closely in those days when she worked alongside her. She came to know Golda the Woman as she had never known anybody before—a woman who hardly took time out to wash her gray hair with its tiny bun on top. Golda's hairdrier left much to be desired. It was a faulty thing that didn't work as often as it did. Lou Kaddar learned that, to Golda personally, peace meant a little more time for everyday things such as washing her hair as often as she liked. Her miserable old hairdrier made her swear she would get a new one someday, but she never did.

She also had a teakettle that was never shiny enough for her. She would polish it endlessly to produce a high sheen. She told Lou Kaddar she enjoyed polishing that kettle when she was alone. And if she felt lonely she would polish it twice as hard. There were many days when Golda Meyerson was sad and lonely. The tea-kettle took on a glistening look in those troubled times. The Minister of Labor's job was not a happy one; it brought one too close to misery and despair.

The State of Israel was no bed of roses, either literally and figuratively. But as a cabinet minis-ter, Golda Meyerson had too many concerns to be alone very often. One major concern developed when she received a visitor from the United States—Senator Hubert Humphrey, who came to Israel's *kibbutzim* to see first hand how they were run. Golda was glad to go on an inspection tour with the senator, with four male and female teachers along for moral and vocal support. These teachers were the life force of the *kibbut-zim;* from them all knowledge, care and training would come for the children.

Senator Humphrey, a volatile, cheery-faced man with a decidedly American flavor to his voice and demeanor, expressed his approval of the *kibbutzim* in no uncertain terms. He did not mince words, this man from America—a man who would one day run for the high office of President of his country and then bravely fight a losing battle against cancer. But that day in

Israel, Hubert Humphrey was a life force for good and progress. Golda listened to what he had to say; he made very good sense.

"I must say I'm impressed by what these teachers are accomplishing with retarded children. You know, I have a particular interest in special education because I have a grandchild who is similarly afflicted."

"Yes, so I understand, Senator."

"But may I ask a question on a different subject, possibly a little sensitive?"

They had all paused in their walk, close to the picnic area with its tables and chairs set out in the bright open sunlight.

"Certainly."

"What about these young couples living together who aren't married?" Golda Meyerson flinched. She gestured to the picnic table nearby. "Would you like to sit down, Senator Humphrey?" He nodded and moved to the table and they sat down facing each other. The teachers joined them, sitting around like a conclave. Senator Humphrey politely waited for Minister Meyerson to continue.

"You, ah . . . mean to say, it isn't done in America?"

"Not so openly," he conceded frankly. "Cohabitation without benefit of clergy is considered scandalous, especially in Middle America where I come from. So I'd be interested in what your attitude is."

Golda Meyerson frowned slightly. "Personally I never thought much about it. To me the main

185

thing would be whether the people love each other."

"Oh, Mrs. Meyerson!" Hubert Humphrey protested, as if he thought that naive. "The main thing is the children!"

"The children?" she echoed weakly.

"Of course!" he snapped. "What happens to the children of those couples? Are they accepted by your society or are they stigmatized? Are they legally legitimate or are they bastards?"

For a moment Golda felt she had met her male counterpart, this man spoke so clearly and directly to the point of what he wanted to say. "I don't think that's much of a problem for us," she hedged.

"Why isn't it?" he demanded.

"Couples who aren't married tend not to have children."

She misunderstood the shock on his face until he answered: "But that problem is even worse! Your country *needs* to increase its population, doesn't it?"

"Desperately," she agreed, a light dawning in her mind.

"And a whole sector of your strongest and healthiest young people refuse to help. Think about that for a moment."

God bless the man! She thought and, in a few seconds, she found herself saying, "Senator, you're absolutely right."

It had taken an outsider, a man from another land and another world, to show her a simple, undeniable truth.

Senator Hubert Humphrey of the United States of America—common sense, hard-hitting, straight-to-the-point America, which knew a little something about Wars for Independence.

Eli and Ruth were both about twenty. They shared a one-room apartment in the *kibbutz*. Golda Meyerson chose them as the first couple on whom to try Senator Humphrey's suggestion. Why not? Eli and Ruth were lovers and Israelis. They *ought* to have children. They had lived together and shared the same bed for a long, long time.

But Eli, dark haired, dark eyed, was resentful when Mrs. Golda Meyerson paid him and Ruth a surprise visit and hinted at some question she wanted to ask them. After all, Golda was the Labor Minister. Anything might be on her mind— anything at all!

"Well, ah . . . what . . . ah . . . kind of question are you asking?"

"A very simple question. Nothing complicated, Eli."

Ruth had placed Golda in the one good chair and served her a cup of tea. But she was wary, too. Something had to be in the wind.

"Do you love each other?" Golda asked them, pointblank.

"Of course we do," Eli blurted quickly.

"So why don't you get married?" the Labor Minister asked.

Eli and Ruth exchanged glances and then stared back at her. Ruth steeled herself for speech and then said: "Look, we know who we are and what our commitment is. We don't need a piece of paper to tell us."

Golda shook her head.

"You love each other. You have a commitment to each other. What would be so wrong with getting married?"

Eli backed off a little. "Nobody says there's anything wrong with it. But nobody's going to push us into it."

"Push you into it? Who would do such a thing?" Golda Meyerson smiled her charming smile. "Let me ask you . . . do you like this room you're living in?"

Ruth's expression spoke volumes. "Not very much."

"I thought not. Too close to the chickens." Golda laughed warmly, remembering *Kibbutz Merhavia* and the first hopeful days. And being young, and Morris Meyerson . . . and those terrible chickens she had had to pluck endlessly. But she shook the memory off. "Would you like to be assigned a room near the flowers?"

"Hah!" Ruth snorted, her pretty face grimacing. "Would we!"

"I can arrange it. And what about this icebox that drips on the floor? I'm sure you wouldn't mind an electric frig. I can arrange that, too." She brushed her hands together with finality.

Eli scowled at her. "What's the catch?"

"Catch? No catch? All I ask in return is what you yourselves say there's nothing wrong with—" she paused—"getting married."

188

The young couple looked at each other. Slowly, tenderly, their little smiles started. Ruth turned back to Golda Meyerson. "Would you come to the wedding, Golda?"

Golda Mabovitch Meyerson did, with a smile on her face and joy in her heart. This was a beginning, a good beginning. But an end was coming that she had not foreseen. It happened when she was temporarily out of Israel. It was 1951 and Morris Meyerson died very suddenly. His heart had given out.

Golda Meyerson flew back for the funeral, in time to see the open grave in the sun-splashed cemetery, to hear the bearded *rabbi* solemnly intone the mourner's *Kaddish*, the Prayer for the Dead. The Prayer for Morris Meyerson.

"*Yisgadal v'yiskkadash sh'meh rabbah. . . .*"

Several dozen mourners surrounded the grave, the three principal ones being two women and a man: Mrs. Golda Meyerson and her son and daughter, Menachem and Sarah, now sturdy young Jewish trees in their twenties. Death had brought together the people that life could not. Morris Meyerson might have smiled to see it, if he could have.

"*. . . B'almah divrah kiruseh v'yamlich malchuseh, b'chayechon uv'yomechon uv'chayeh d'chol bes yisroel. . . .*"

Golda's mind and memory was assailed with images, reflections, shadows, turmoil. She recalled her life with Morris Meyerson, from the very beginning. And even as the rabbi spoke the *Kaddish*, her conscience seemed to speak aloud, heedless of all that was going on around her.

"I remember thinking, as though it weren't too late to tell him, 'Dear Morris, I loved you so when we were young. Things changed for us, but in a way they stayed the same. I never lost the feeling for you. Never.'" She thought about how he had loved the children, and they had adored him, too. Menachim wasn't married now, but Sarah was. And she had a little girl, a lovely little thing.

"Morris, at least we can be glad that Sarah's marriage is working out better than ours."

Golda Meyerson stood rigid, head down, between her children as the rabbi droned on. The tears in her eyes were like frozen drops. "But mainly I kept thinking how very sad he was, the last years of his life. And I was to blame, because I could always get him to do pretty much what I wanted, but I couldn't be the wife he wanted and should have had. In the end, whatever I was able to accomplish, Morris Meyerson paid for."

" . . . *Oseh sholom bimromov, hu ya'aseh sholom. Olenu v'al kol yisroel, v'yimru ohmen. . . .*"

The *Kaddish* ended on a note of Hebrew fervor. Everyone present chorused *Ohmen!* the Jewish equivalent of amen.

Mrs. Meyerson stepped forward alone, to the freshly heaped dirt beside the grave. She picked up a handful of the sod and began to toss it into the open grave below her. The tiny pebbles rattled with finality on the sacred shroud which covered the last earthly remains of Morris Meyerson, sign painter. The pebbles were another Hebrew custom.

"*Shalom*, Morris," Golda whispered, and turned away, the frozen tears now thawed, running down her lined face. Morris Meyerson was gone from her life forever.

Golda Mabovitch Meyerson remained Israel's Labor Minister for seven long years, and Lou Kaddar stayed at her side all the way. Golda was doing what she loved best, working with people to provide the solid things that people needed— like housing. All this while the Arab-Jewish hostilities continued. Israel was like an armed camp. A rifle shot could always kill an unwary Jew, or a careless one.

Golda knew of things that could turn a desert into a place worth living in. One of those things was trees, and she planted some of them herself in the Herzl Memorial Forest—ceremoniously planting little seedlings, handling the fragile plants as though they were babies. Jerusalem Park was another project. And there Golda Mabovitch Meyerson could always be seen, wheeling one grandchild in a pram, while another grandchild trotted alongside. Israel whispered that Mrs. Meyerson had become a doting grandmother, the typical Jewish archetype, because she was trying to make up for not having been a doting Jewish mother to her own children. Perhaps that was true. Who knows for certain? Golda, in her heart of hearts, supposed that Israel was right. She could never rid herself of the feelings of guilt in regard to Menachem and Sarah, and Morris Meyerson. In any case, between the joy that the children gave her and the satisfaction of doing her job, these were proving to be the beautiful years, the best years of her life. She grew older gracefully.

And Lou Kaddar, faithful, hard-working Lou, was happy for her. But soon it was 1955 and, with the appearance of a man named Gamal Abdal Nasser, there came an end to these beautiful years. Israel was in great trouble. Armageddon had once more come.

Colonel-President Nassar of Egypt instructed all his soldiers, and his *fedayeen*, to dedicate themselves to the killing of Jews and drive them out of the Land of the Pyramids forever. A new blood bath began in earnest. *Death to all those who wore the Star of David!* The Gaza Strip became an international headline. It was a roadway of destruction and annihilation for Jews.

Cairo Radio made Nasser's intent official. Colonel Gamal Abdal Nasser, Egypt's new President, sent terror squads called *fedayeen* to stage indiscriminate attacks, such as the horrible killing of six children and their teacher in an agricultural school. The *fedayeen* operated from bases around Israel's borders. And to dispel all doubts, Cairo Radio send the message out to the world loud and clear. The terrible words, originally in Arabic, when translated for outsiders, were doom laden and chilling.

"*Weep, O Israel, the day of your extermination draws near! We have found the way to strike you.*

There will be no more arguments at the United Nations. There will be no peace. We demand the death of Israel."

The world shuddered, the world was outraged, but Israel was the one that had to live with this threat and fight it.

Nasser was not fooling. He meant every word, this hawk-nosed, brown-faced hater of the children of Israel, this son of Egypt. And in the Israeli Parliament, the *Knesset*, Nasser put some of his desires for Egypt into action. The entire universe heard about the hand grenade and the would-be assassin in the gallery who stood up and threw it.

David Ben-Gurion, Golda Meyerson and other eminent officials were seated at the cabinet table going over the order of business. The grenade, egg shaped, awesome, came down from the gallery, thrown by the man who had leaped to his feet, face contorted and maniacally purposeful. The grenade skipped along the polished floor and settled before the cabinet table directly in front of David Ben-Gurion. A woman screamed, but it was not Golda Meyerson. She was too busy at the moment for shock or fear. She rose quickly at sight of the grenade, and sprang at David Ben-Gurion, carrying him and his chair to the floor. The other officials were reacting with frenzied speed, but no one could stop that flung grenade from exploding. The five seconds were up. Golda covered the startled Ben-Gurion with her body.

There was a roar, a flash and a thunderous burst of violence. The *Knesset* turned into a scene

193

of bedlam and pandemonium. Nasser's long, angry arm had reached into the Parliament of the Jews, and the world now knew he meant every word of his pronunciamento of death to the Jews.

Uniformed policemen stood outside Golda Meyerson's hospital-room door. They saluted David Ben-Gurion as he hurried past a plump nurse carrying a meal tray. Ben-Gurion's face was a study in concern. He entered the room to find Mrs. Meyerson sitting up in bed, one leg propped up. A clutter of papers surrounded her. She had obviously been working again, in spite of all that had happened that morning.

"So," Ben-Gurion, as crusty as ever, mocked, "can I believe what they told me? You're all right?"

"I'll be back in my office tomorrow, if I live. If not, I'll be back the day after." The famous Jewish joke made them both laugh. Ben-Gurion sat in the chair next to the bed. Golda eyed him affectionately.

"Listen, Golda, speaking of living . . . I never mentioned it while your husband was alive. But you, of all people, haven't taken a Hebrew name."

"I don't see any reason to change Meyerson," she answered loyally.

Ben-Gurion made a face. "It's policy. All government officials are expected to have Hebrew names—especially someone with your high visibility outside of Israel, which is going to be even higher now."

She misunderstood him, thinking that he was

referring to her bravery in the Knesset. "What is this, B-G?"

"Moshe Sharett is leaving the cabinet to be Secretary-General of the Labor Party."

"But who'll be foreign minister?"

"You," he said, curtly.

She was completely astonished and taken aback for once.

"Oh, no. No. I don't believe you can mean such a thing."

"Of course I mean it," he growled at her.

"No, no!" She shook her head vehemently. "In the first place I don't want to leave the Labor Ministry! That's my kind of work! The Foreign Ministry is full of . . . of sophisticated intellectuals with Oxford and Cambridge educations. How would I fit in with them?"

"You will make them fit in with you," he insisted, brooking no argument from her. "I know you will. Somebody asked me how I could pick a woman to be foreign minister and I said, 'Golda is the best man in my cabinet.'"

She wagged her head. "You'll excuse me, B-G, if I'm not wild about the compliment."

He grinned at her. "Fine. Don't be wild. But don't be your usual stubborn self, either. You are taking over as foreign minister, and that's that."

The Prime Minister had spoken. Golda gaped. "I'm stubborn?"

But the issue was closed. Ben-Gurion was thinking of something else already. "Now about changing your name. I thought of one that's close to Meyerson . . . Meir. A fine Hebrew word meaning to illuminate, shed light. You should give this serious consideration."

She was defeated by him as usual. "Anything else I should do?" she asked drily.

"Yes. You should understand that it's not in my nature to make a fuss over what you did for me, much as I appreciate it."

Gently she smiled. "Don't you think I know that?"

Ben-Gurion continued, "And one more thing, No argument this time, please. I want you to take a little better care of yourself. Don't be in a hurry to come back to work. Go to some nice hotel on the seashore. Rest. Relax. Let your leg heal. Caesarea is a lovely place."

"No argument, B-G. I'll do exactly as you say."

Lou Kaddar had been begging her for weeks to take a vacation. And now, B-G himself—

He had paused on his way out the door, smiling, turning to say, "A week should be more than enough."

After the door closed Golda Mabovitch Meyerson, now Golda Meir, fell to laughing heartily, before the laughter turned to sober sadness again. It had been another golden moment, being named foreign minister of Israel.

The little girl from Kiev, Russia, had come a long, long way. And, unknown to herself, she was to go even further. The best was yet to come, even though bigger troubles would come with it. There was always trouble when you were born Jewish.

Had it not always been so?

## *Ideals*

---

The gentle waves lapped at the stretch of sand
along the beach. The great Roman aqueduct
*Caesarea* filled the blue horizon. Here Israelis
invariably vacationed, as surcease from the daily
ferment of Jewish life in the desert. Golda Meir
and Efraim Ben-Ariel, two people who deserved a
vacation more than most, lolled in the sun,
basking comfortably. They had brought a blanket and a picnic hamper but neither of them was
very hungry. Ariel was still very upset by the
recent change in Israel's fortunes. Egypt and
Nasser had darkened the blue sky for all Jews
everywhere.

"I was surprised to see this terrible business
get such skimpy coverage in the news that you
weren't even mentioned. They told me you wanted the story kept quiet," Ariel said.

"Why not? Do I need a medal?"

"They say you also help to suppress *fedayeen*
terrorist stories, like when they bombed the
wedding party in the Negev village, and when

they killed the archeologists working on the dig near Ramat Rachel." His tone was accusing.

"It's not a good idea to make heroes out of murderers. It helps them attract imitators, Ariel."

"It's not a good idea for a government to manage the news too much, either."

"Ariel," she said, patiently, "what did you come out here for?"

As if in answer, he rose from the blanket and placed a brown hand on the ancient stones surrounding them. As he gazed at the rising wall behind them, his smile was tolerant.

"Maybe I came to admire the aqueduct. It's one of the wonders of the ancient world."

She shook her head. "Really, Ariel?"

"Sure it is," he said with deliberate malice. "Built by the Romans in the second century, it carried sweet spring water all the way from the mountains by the Sea of Galilee."

The graceful arches and columns were splendid, true. Not even the decay of time could detract from their magnificence. Ariel added, "Or maybe I came to sit by the beautiful Mediterranean—" he turned to the shining sea, limned in the sunlight— "and forget what life is like here." He sat down beside her once more. "Almost," he ended bitterly.

"Almost," Golda repeated slowly.

At the crest of the aqueduct two Israeli soldiers stood watch. Both were older reservists, armed with rifles. One was scanning the sea with binoculars. Ariel picked up a handful of sand and let it filter through his fingers. Golda

198

watched him concernedly.

"Exactly. One of the archeologists killed on that dig was my father-in-law."

She felt a rush of pity and sorrow. "Oh, Ariel. I didn't know."

"Doctor Walter Rubin, Gabi's father."

Golda touched his arm and squeezed consolingly. He nodded, appreciating that. "Life here . . . is so damn hard . . . it takes a certain kind of person to hold up. A person like you, or me. But Gabi is not that kind. She gives me the feeling that she's just about hanging on by her fingernails. That's why I've never been able to bring myself to ask her for a divorce."

"I've understood that for a long time."

"How?" he marveled.

"I felt the same way about Morris."

"Have you heard the joke that's going around?" He chuckled bitterly. One man says, 'Yes, it's great that the Jewish people have their own country after two thousand years—"

"'But why did it have to happen to me?'" Golda finished. Ariel laughed and she laughed. Their voices blended, with the low murmur of the waves as counterpoint. Then they fell into a silent, serious moment. Suddenly Ariel stirred.

"Let's stay the weekend, Golda. Never mind when Ben-Gurion thinks you're coming back."

Golda Meir smiled fully on the face of the man she loved. "Ben who?" she asked mischievously.

Ariel's answering smile was like the sun coming up over Mount Sinai. He whooped with delight, going to her, taking both her hands in his own. Love shone in his warm eyes.

Life in the desert, whatever it was, was meant to be lived, wasn't it? Especially by the likes of Golda Meir and Efraim Ben-Ariel—two extraordinary Jewish people, titans of the struggle for survival.

Almost as soon as Golda Mabovitch Meyerson became Golda Meir and Israel's second foreign minister, she inherited the problem of Israel's second war. The Arabs and their leaders had never accepted peace. And Golda Meir, mounting to the podium in the United Nations to take her post of office officially, could not change that. The members of the UN, even as they applauded Golda Meir, did so with a sense of doom in their reaction. Nasser of Egypt was very close to throttling the Israeli state in its infancy, with guns, terror and inhumanity.

The President of Egypt had nationalized the Suez Canal and had closed it to all Israeli ships. His shore batteries in the Sinai prevented all ships from reaching Israel's port city of Eilat. His *fedayeen* attacks continued, unabated.

He was staging a massive military buildup with weapons supplied by the Soviet Union. These weapons that were the latest and best in the art of technological death—tanks, aircraft, cannon, land mines.

Against all this, Israel countered with a motley assortment of equipment and personnel. Its tanks were followed by trucks, buses, private cars, taxis, milk trucks and, incredibly, ice-cream vehicles.

On October 29, 1956, under the command of Chief-of-Staff Moshe Dayan, the Israeli Army—mostly reservists in a weird collection of vehicles—crossed into the Sinai Peninsula. Major Orde Wingate, had he been present, would have been very proud of these Jews whom he had once trained in the arts of war. Dayan's army, such as it was, took the Gaza Strip, plus the entire Sinai, in less than a hundred hours. The world, watching, could scarcely believe its eyes. Mighty Egypt and Nasser had been thrown back.

But in the United Nations Assembly, as Golda Meir addressed the membership, military victory was transformed into political defeat. Israel came under intense pressure to withdraw from her takeover.

The sixty-year-old woman standing before the UN Assembly, with reading glasses perched on her shapely nose, was compelled to take the only road left open to Israel by this Assembly. "And in response to United Nations guarantees of freedom of navigation for Israeli ships and all shipping in the Gulf of Aqaba, and an end to terrorist raids, my government is prepared to announce plans for a full and prompt withdrawal from the Sinai and the Gaza Strip."

As she took off her glasses the Assembly applauded, thinly. Tiredly, she rubbed the bridge of her nose. Politics, wheeling-and-dealing, diplomacy . . . it was an endless go-round from sunup to sundown. Where would it all end for her country, her Israel?

It came back to her then, that day at the Israeli army base where she was guarded by soldiers overseen by Moshe Dayan. The tents held prisoners of war. Dayan, spirited and warriorlike as ever, had asked her, "Do you want to go into this one? It's for Egyptian prisoners."

"If you're going, I'll go too."

He had led her into the big tent. Surprisingly, it was a hospital tent. The wounded Egyptians were being tended to by the Israeli medical staff. There was a narrow aisle between two rows of cots. Moshe Dayan walked her to a particular one, where an Egyptian prisoner lay. The man had a thick bandage over one eye. Dayan himself had by now the black patch which would eternally show on his weathered face for the world to see, a memento of battle. He had lost his left eye during fighting for the British in Lebanon— fighting courageously, as always.

"*Salaam*," Dayan said to the wounded Egyptian. "*Aleykum*."

"*Sholom aleichim*," the prisoner replied. "I speak Hebrew."

"Good. Then I can give you some classified information." He sat on the cot and smiled at the prisoner. Golda looked on wonderingly, not knowing what Dayan was up to.

"For whatever is worth seeing," Moshe Dayan said, "in this miserable world, one eye is enough."

The Egyptian smiled gratefully through his bandage. He reached gropingly for his enemy's hand.

"Thank you for the information, brother." He squeezed Moshe Dayan's hand. "Brother. We are brothers."

Golda Meir was deeply moved. And as she looked up again at the Assembly faces before her, she spoke without notes. "May I add these few words to the neighbors of Israel? Can we, now, for all of us, turn over a new leaf? Can we act like brothers and sisters should? Instead of fighting each other, can we fight poverty, disease, illiteracy? Hatred will never make one child in your countries happier. The implements of death will never convert one hovel into a house. Isn't it possible for us to put our efforts, our energies, into one single purpose—the betterment of all our lands and all our people, through the blessings of peace?"

There was barely any response from the membership, only a smattering of perfunctory handclapping—a courtesy, really.

The polite applause was all right, but there was no reaction from the Arab delegates. Golda Meir knew in her heart and mind that there would be no peace. The Israeli soldiers who had fought and died had only bought a little precious time, a breathing space of questionable length. Israel would have to fight again, as it had had to do since someone threw the first stone at a Jew. *Kaddishes* would be intoned all over Israel in the days to come. This truce was no *mitzvah* at all; far from it.

The years of ordeal swept by.

Golda Meir, foreign minister, was kept very busy, both in her own country and abroad, as the intermittent fighting and trouble went on. As Israel's First Lady of sorts, she remained in the eyes of the world. She went to Paris to meet President Charles De Gaulle. She went to Washington to meet President Eisenhower. She went to Ottawa, Canada to meet that country's Prime Minister. In Lima, Peru, she spoke of Israel to thousands of people. Emperor Hirohito of Japan welcomed her once. In Manila, she received a degree. She paused at a Burmese temple; she talked with Haile Selassie of Ethiopia. All in all, she talked to just about everybody who was prominent in the strife-torn world of the late Fifties and early Sixties.

At that time there was only woman foreign minister on earth, and almost everyone could have told you her name was Golda Meir. Lou Kaddar traveled with her to the capitals of Europe, to the United States and Canada, to Latin America, Japan, the Philippines, Burma and Ethiopia, among other places. Lou Kaddar believed that, of all the continents Golda Meir visited, Golda herself felt she had accomplished the most in Africa.

Darkest Africa, where civilization had never gotten a firm foothold; where Golda Meir of Israel danced the *hora* with natives wearing African dress. The music was louder but somehow different. Golda Meir, earth woman, earth mother, was among friends, people who understood her and what she was trying to say and do.

In Zoe Village of Ghana, Golda was able to set up a program for thousands of Africans to come to Israel to study subjects like hydrology and agriculture. And thousands of Israeli doctors, engineers, technical specialists and experts would come to Africa in exchange.

Lou Kaddar would take with her to her grave the memory of one particular day in that African village, when Golda Meir, surrounded by black journalists and Israeli security men, was interviewed by the press. A circle of folding chairs had been set on the cleared earth and here Golda Meir held court in her usual, winning way.

One black newspaperman was very cold and tough to her. "Mrs. Meir, my question is, why is Israel going to this considerable expense for a program such as you suggest?"

"Israel is a small, poor nation that has learned some hard lessons about economic and social developments. We feel a responsibility to share what we've learned with other small, poor nations."

The frank answer did not seem to please the black journalist.

"Mrs. Meir, that sounds very nice. But I'm from Algeria. Your country is being armed by France, the country that is fighting a brutal, ruthless war against us. How do you justify your intimacy with a power that is the enemy of self-determination for African people?"

Golda was on the spot and she knew it, so she paused to light one of her cigarettes. The newspapermen waited for her answer.

"Our neighbors are out to destroy us," she replied slowly. "They are getting up-to-date weapons from the Soviet Union, free of charge. Most of our friends, for whatever reasons, won't sell us arms. The only country that will sell to us—and for a lot of hard currency—is France. If President De Gaulle were the Devil himself, I would expect my government to buy from him what we need to defend ourselves." She stared up at the hostile, hard-eyed journalist. "And if you were in that position, sir, what in the name of God would you do?"

Everyone was silent for a long moment, thinking over her answer and her defense. Finally, with a Gallic shrug, the Algerian journalist smiled. "Madame, at least you live up to your publicity, which says you are honest to a fault."

Everybody laughed, but the laughter was interrupted by the abrupt beating of drums and the thumping of hands on leather hide. Soon a pair of black women came running, encircling Golda Meir and laying hands on her. Lou Kaddar was alarmed and started forward to protest. "You come!" the black women chorused as one. "Come now! Come!" Golda signaled Lou Kaddar and the security men, strapping ex-paratroopers, to stay back. It was all right with her. The journalists looked on as the two black women hurried Golda Meir from her chair, taking her off with them toward one of the huge thatched huts.

Lou Kaddar and the security men followed, in helpless confusion. It was Golda Meir's party, but— A man called Irving, in charge of the security, bawled in her wake, "Wait a minute. Just a minute, Mrs. Meir." The ex-paratroopers were reaching for their guns.

"It's all right, Irving," she called back over her shoulder.

"What's all right?" he screamed. "We don't know where they're taking you!"

Golda Meir laughed like a young girl. "Don't worry, Irving."

Tribesmen and tribeswomen could now be seen milling around the thatched reed hut, chanting and singing. The drums kept up a feverish rhythm. Irving, his paratroopers and Lou Kadder could only stand by as the black women led Golda Meir into the huge hut. The drums pounded.

"Mrs. Kaddar, maybe they'll let a woman into that hut. I mean, how do we know what they might do to her?"

Lou Kaddar, as helpless as he was, imitated Golda Meir: "It's all right, Irving. Don't worry."

But the drumbeat grew louder, the time interval grew longer and Golda Meir remained in the large hut. Irving was stewing in fretful silence. Lou Kaddar was worried, too. They had pulled a reed curtain across the entranceway to the hut. Irving looked at his watch constantly. His men matched his worried looks. Golda Meir's safety and well-being was everything to them, to Israel. Mrs. Lou Kadder began to lose her own studied calm. She started for the tent curtain. And then the incessant drums stopped, the beat ended and a great cheer went up from the natives behind them, watching the hut. Lou Kadder saw with her own eyes the miracle before her. So did Irving and his security men. A goddess had stepped from the tent into plain view.

No one would have recognized the foreign minister of Israel.

In flamboyant headdress and African tribal robes, Golda Meir strode from the hut, walking like a queen. Feathers and bright colors clothed her. Lou Kaddar, Irving and the security men gaped. A live white chicken was held by one of the black handmaidens. Golda Meir shouted, "Can you believe this could happen to little Golda Mabovitch of Kiev and Pinsk and Milwaukee?" There was awe in her tone.

"*What* happened?" a stunned Lou Kaddar asked.

"I am now a member of the Secret Society of Zoe Tribeswomen, the only foreign woman they have ever admitted. Lou, I must have a picture for my grandchildren!"

"We'll take pictures, Golda. But what went on in that hut?"

The newest member of the Secret Society of Zoe Tribeswomen smiled craftily. "Lou, it's a secret society. It was a secret ceremony. I will never tell."

And she never did.

Now she walked, with majestic slowness, away from Lou Kaddar, in her tribal robes and headdress. Irving and the security men gawked after her like autograph hounds watching a movie star.

Somewhere in the midst of all this travel, travail and excitement, Golda Meir managed a candlelit supper for two with Ariel, her Ariel whom the world knew as Efraim Ben-Ariel. There was much to talk about, much to remember, much to tell Ariel about.

"And what do you think he wanted then?"

"Are we still talking about Idi Amin?"

They were dining in one of the better restaurants in Tel Aviv. The walls were stucco, the *decor* simple, but the food always excellent. And they were among friends; everyone in the place knew them.

"Yes, yes. Idi Amin, that *meshuganah.* When I said I couldn't give him six fighter planes, he asked for ten million pounds sterling. I couldn't help laughing."

"Golda—" Ariel looked as if he wanted to talk about something else. But she hurried on.

"Then he threatened to go to our enemies, meaning Libya. I should have handled it better in some way."

"Golda, don't you ever chat?"

"What?" She blinked at that.

"Chat. Make small talk. Over coffee, especially. You never do."

She stared at him, offended, as he sipped his wine. "You want to chat? *Nu,* chat! Chat!"

Ariel laughed, put down his glass, and stared at her earnestly. "Gabi wants a divorce," he offered.

The disclosure astonished her. For a moment her tongue stalled. Then: "Really? When did this happen?"

"She just told me. Actually it happened a few months ago, when she met a man who recently immigrated—an American. Gabi feels she could be a lot happier with him than she is with me."

"Well, that's a surprise." She shook her head. "And?"

"And if Gabi has a chance to be happy, by all means she should take it. And I think you should have the same chance, Golda." He paused a moment. "As soon as the divorce comes through, will you marry me?"

Her hand went to her throat as if he had taken her breath away. He certainly had.

"Oh, that's not fair!" she murmured.

"What isn't fair?"

"You say chat, and then . . . is this a subject for chatting?"

Ariel shrugged. "Compared to Idi Amin—" He stared at her, long and hard. "What's the answer?"

Golda Meir could not take her eyes off his dear face. "Ariel, I don't know what to say. I have to sleep on it. I have to wash my hair and think. We both have such important work. Would being married interfere? And is it too late for us, anyway? Are we too old?"

"What's with this 'too old'?" he chided her affectionately. "I'm not proposing to crawl through barbed wire. I'm just proposing." She had lapsed into a moody silence. "Golda, stop thinking of your work and think of yourself for a change, before it really is too late."

She could only look at him and smile at him tenderly, thoughtfully, remembering all the years that had gone by for them both. Her silence seemed almost like a promise to Ariel. He took her hands and touched her fingertips with his own.

The love in the atmosphere between them was thick enough to cut with a knife. In the *Sanhedrin* of the Talmud there is a line: "When love is strong, a man and woman can make their bed on a sword's blade; when love is weak, a bed of sixty cubits is not wide enough." Golda and Ariel had had the strong love since the very beginning.

The next day dawned bright and clear. Another promise.

The polished teakettle in Golda Meir's kitchen was whistling furiously. Golda hurried in from the living room, wrapping a towel around her freshly washed hair. She took the kettle, poured herself a cup of hot tea and then surveyed the kettle with an "Eh" as if it could be polished even more than it was. But her attitude now was go-to-hellish; she was happy, excited. Ariel's news had opened up a whole new world of possibilities to her. The phone rang. She knew now what her answer to Ariel's proposal would be: yes, most definitely yes!

The caller was Lou Kaddar. "Hello . . . good morning, Lou . . . beautiful day . . . no, it won't be too hot. Just perfect! Lou, dear, would you please have the car brought a little early this morning? I have a breakfast appointment with, ah . . . with someone. Seven-thirty. Fine. Thank you."

She hung up and took the tea into the bath-room. Unwrapping the towel with one hand, with the other she reached for the old hairdrier and flipped the switch. Nothing happened. Golda Meir laughed. It did not matter; Efraim Ben-Ariel had asked her to marry him.

But she got the darn thing working anyway, and that too augured well for the day. She felt as if a new life was dawning for her.

She was singing happily as the drier *whirred* into her wet hair.


When her private limousine arrived at Ariel's apartment house, the sun was in its heaven but all was not right with the Israeli world. An ambulance was drawn to the curbside, and peo-ple were gathering excitedly to watch the white-coated attendants opening the loading door.

Golda Meir did not notice or see the ambulance. Her eyes were on the small sidewalk cafe down the block where she was to meet Ariel. A waiter, expecting her, waved her to one of the tables. There Golda saw the setting for two, with a single rose and a newspaper already placed. Her heart full of joy and anticipation, she did not see the man who suddenly came from across the street and approached her where she was sitting, looking at the newspaper. "Mrs. Meir. . . ."

She looked up, not recognizing the man, whose face was a study in mixed emotions. "Yes?"

"My name is Kedem. I'm the manager of the apartment building. . . ." He gestured down the block. Golda smiled pleasantly at this. "Yes?" she said again.

"Mr. Ariel introduced us once."

"Ah, yes. I know you now, Mr. Kedem."

All at once she was aware of the excitement on the Jerusalem street—the ambulance, the crowd of people, the activity. Her heart leaped. Ariel—Kedem's eyes were forlorn.

"Tell me what happened," Golda Meir said quickly.

"We don't know, yet . . . maybe a heart attack. Mr. Ariel asked the switchboard for a wakeup call but he didn't answer, so I went up and opened the door. It looked as if he must have died as soon as he went into the apartment last night." Kedem trailed off helplessly. Mrs. Meir looked like a stone statue, hearing the awful news.

The deep, draining, freezing shock of his words had settled over Golda like a block of ice. She could not take her eyes off Mr. Kedem for a long terrible moment. Then she glanced across the street, almost as if she really did not want to look.

A gurney bearing a covered form had just come out of the building. It was being wheeled toward the ambulance, lifted into the interior. The door closed. The crowd stepped back, hushed, respectful. The ambulance drove away with a quiet hiss of tires. Golda watched like a woman in a dream, with the terrible realization that there was nothing she could do now. *Nothing.* She could not even cry.

She returned to her apartment.

She let herself in slowly, like a sleepwalker. Her face was a dead, unmoving mask. She stood for a long moment in the center of the apartment, not knowing what to do or where to turn. Then she walked into the kitchen and took the teakettle down from the shelf. She held it up, turning it, examining it.

She reached into the cabinet over the sink and drew forth a can of metal polish and a cloth. Then she sat down at the kitchen table and began to polish the teakettle. The tears had now come to her eyes and started falling, staining the table before her. She kept on polishing, harder, faster, as though she might never stop. The teakettle began to gleam again.

*Ariel, Ariel, Ariel. . . .*

Golda Meir wept for her dead.

Lou Kaddar recalled all too well the time of Efraim Ben-Ariel's sudden death. For long days after that Golda seemed to be trying to bury herself in her work. Lou thought the idea might have succeeded, but Golda collapsed on several occasions, from what was obviously overexhaustion. She had driven herself too hard in trying to forget.

Worried, Lou Kaddar finally got her to go to the hospital for a complete medical checkup. By the same kind of gentle persuasion Mrs. Meir used on her cabinet colleagues, Lou Kaddar swore up and down she would quit her job if Golda did not go. In the end, Golda went. She saw Dr. Chaim Landau, Chief of Hematology in Hadassah Hos-

214

pital in Jerusalem. A gentle, understated man, Dr. Landau saw her for two visits before he made his final diagnosis. Then he placed his fingers on Golda's neck.

"Those lumps don't mean anything, do they?" Golda asked lightly. Landau did not answer. He pulled his chair closer and seemed to be studying his renowned patient. "They do?" When Landau nodded, she urged him on. "Nu, let's hear."

"What you have, according to the biopsy, is a disease of the lymphatic system called lymphoma. Malignant lymphoma."

"Malignant. I understand, Dr. Landau. It'll spread."

"Eventually it penetrates the other systems."

"How much time do I have?"

"Oh, it's not a rapidly metastasizing condition. I'd say you have a good few years ahead of you."

The stoic, thoughtful look the world had come to see on Golda Meir's face was now visible once more.

"Well, I'm sixty-six. How much longer can I expect to live anyway? The question is, those few years—will they really be good, or will I be suffering?"

Dr. Landau was precise and kind. "There's very little suffering for most of the disease's course, Mrs. Meir. There's not much pain associated with it."

"What about my mind?" she persisted. "I don't want to live one minute after my mind isn't clear."

He smiled tolerantly. "Your mind won't be

215

affected."

"What must I do?" she asked matter-of-factly, clearly relieved.

"Practically nothing. Your motor and sensory abilities are not impaired, so we won't go in for heavy chemotherapy at this time. Just a few simple drugs."

"Drugs?" She bristled. "What drugs? Listen, Doctor, I'm a person who doesn't even like to take aspirin."

He smiled. "We'll discuss each one as we come to it."

"Will they make my hair fall out?" She had heard many scare stories about chemotherapy.

"One or two might, possibly," he hedged.

"No. Absolutely not. I don't care, I won't take any drug that'll make me lose my hair."

"All right," Dr. Landau agreed, "if you feel that way we'll avoid those medications and go to different ones, Mrs. Meir."

"Good. Then I'll trust you—on one condition. If anything about this is ever going to be told to anyone, I will choose who and when. Otherwise it's a strict secret between you and me. Is that agreed, Dr. Landau?"

"Agreed, Mrs. Meir."

Golda Meir nodded, satisfied. Then she said, "Oh, there is one other thing."

"Yes?" Dr. Landau looked puzzled.

"Would it hurt to call me Golda, like everyone else does?"

Lou Kaddar waited outside the hospital, in the

long limousine, with the chauffeur Max. They both looked eager when Golda returned to the car, smiling. Lou wanted to know immediately what the doctor had said. Golda chuckled, nodding as if content.

"Well?" Lou shot at her.

"It's what you said—a slight case of exhaustion."

"That's all?" Lou frowned, suspicious.

"To the office please, Max," Golda told the chauffeur. The long car moved out. "You're not satisfied with your own diagnosis? All right, it's also complications from the shrapnel in my leg."

"And what are you going to do about it?"

"Retire."

Lou reacted with complete surprise. "Golda! You don't mean it!"

"Why don't I?"

"Because! Come on, Golda, are you serious? Can you see yourself out of politics, much less retired?"

Thinking that one over, with a bittersweet smile tugging at her mouth corners, Golda murmured, "Yes, I can see myself . . . with books that I've been wanting to read. Going to the theater, to movies—you know I like the movies. And I can see myself with my grandchildren, spending time I could never spend with my own children. Not looking at my watch—do I have to go?—the way I'm rushing now. Why not, Lou? Must I always be the woman who doesn't stop working?"

Sympathetic as always, but still skeptical, still

suspicious, Lou Kaddar looked straight ahead. "Ben-Gurion is retiring—that's enough of a loss to the country for awhile. They say Levi Eshkol will replace him. Is that right?"

"Probably," Golda said.

"What will you do when Eshkol asks you to stay on? Which he most certainly will. Are you going to desert a brand-new Prime Minister of your own party?" Lou Kaddar hurled that at her like a challenge.

There it was again. Don't think of yourself, Golda Meir. Think of the good of your country. Think of Israel. Think of—

Golda rubbed her eyes wearily, reflecting, pondering, thinking over what Lou had said. It would be a shame to desert Eshkol if he needed her. But—

"It's less than two years to the next elections. I suppose if Eshkol says he needs me, I'll stay on that long. But no longer. Time is too precious to me now."

That was the end of the subject for the time being. They finished the car ride in silence. The matter was closed.

But Golda Meir stayed on as foreign minister for two more years before she resigned and was succeeded in the job by Abba Eban. Her retirement did not last very long, though.

In Northern Israel, among the green mountains, some snow showed on the highest tors. And on the Golan Heights in Syria, from commanding positions, Syrian artillery, supplied by the Soviet Union, shelled mercilessly the Israeli villages across the border, below. One of the worst attacks was on the *kibbutz* of Gadot.

It was spring of 1967, and the long guns of Syria completely decimated the *kibbutz* with their murderous artillery. And Golda Meir found out that she was needed again—needed as she never had been before, not even in the old days. The word came from Eshkol himself—Levi Eshkol, a good man, the Prime Minister of Israel.

# Renaissance

The *kibbutz* of Gadot was devastated—burned out school bus, shattered buildings with the smoke still rising, ruined rubble everywhere the eye could see, the debris of annihilation and wholesale destruction. Small crowds had gathered, to essay the damage and look for survivors; a piteous wailing was going up all over. Uniformed soldiers tried to help the demoralized *kibbutzniks.* In the middle of the milling people two men stood, the center of the storm and strife. These were Moshe Dayan, his famous black eyepatch marking him for all time, and Levi Eshkol, the Prime Minister. Neither of them was very happy. Syria's artillery from the Golan Heights had scored direct hit after direct hit. The dead had not yet been counted or determined. When the car horn sounded suddenly, blasting through the din of aftermath, Levi Eshkol looked up and recognized Golda Meir's limousine, with Max at the wheel. Eshkol hurried to it, meeting Golda as she emerged from the vehicle.

Eshkol held the door for her in silent greeting, then took her hand and led her toward the flamed-out bus which stood, tilted, smoldering, and gestured that she should step up and look inside. She did so, with a pang in her heart. The bodies of the busload had already been removed but the shambles of the wreckage spoke for them all too vividly. Golda trembled. Eshkol said emphatically, "Twenty people died in there. Then there are the people in five houses that were hit by shells. . . ." She stared at him in disbelief. Grimly he continued, "Plus the kindergarten building and the nurseries. Total casualties. . . ."

"Stop, Eshkol," she begged, overburdened with sorrow. "Stop. I don't want to know any more."

Moshe Dayan had joined them. He found Golda weeping, as much in anger as in sorrow. Dayan kept his peace as Golda whirled on Eshkol. He had never seen her so openly moved, so openly angry.

"Why . . . why did I have to see this, Eshkol? I'm retired. I'm a private citizen. It's bad enough that I had to hear it on the radio. Why did you send a car for me? I have my own."

"Because," Levi Eshkol said pointedly, "I want you to have a very clear picture of what's happening. I want you to hear it from Dayan." He moved out of the way so Moshe could speak to her face to face.

"Golda, in addition to the threat from Syria, Jordan is filling up with Iraqi forces, including pilots and planes. The King of Jordan just placed his army under the command of an Egyptian

222

general. Egypt now has as many troops along our border as in Fifty-six—and more tanks."

"But there is a very big difference," she argued back. "This time there are United Nations troops between, as a buffer."

Dayan winced. "Nassar ordered the UN out."

"They won't leave!" she shouted. "The UN gave us guarantees!"

"They *are* leaving!" Dayan shouted back. "Our observation planes spotted them at first light this morning! The UN is moving out!"

Levi Eshkol sighed wearily, in confirmation.

"As soon as they're gone, Nasser will close the straits and choke off Eilat again. He says so. If we accept all this, we might as well cut our throats as they did in Masada centuries ago. Remember?"

Golda Meir absorbed all this horror in one minute. It was unspeakable, but she knew it was true. She also knew what she had to do.

"Tell me how I can help," she said in her simple, direct way.

"Come back to work," Eshkol said gently. "We need you."

"Where? Abba Eban is running the foreign ministry very well."

"I'm not saying run the foreign ministry. I'm saying—run the party. If you were secretary-general, you could unite the party like nobody else. The majority party must stand united now." He looked at her with steel in his eye. "What do you say, Golda?"

What could she say, after having seen the burned-out bus, the shelled kindergarten, the

223

nurseries, the countless dead?

"Of course," she said, very quietly.

Israel needed her again, as it always had. Who could say no to Israel? Golda Meir had never learned how. Now she was secretary-general of Israel's ruling party, another giant step upward on the country's ladder.

In Golda Meir's Labor Party office, there was no such thing as a slow day. Events piled up, things happened, the war headlines grew larger as the Israeli-Egyptian hostilities stepped up. The new role for Golda was another challenge, one she had accepted unwillingly but, as was her custom, tackled with everything she had in her.

One thing she did, as soon as she could, was to phone the Revivim *kibbutz* where her daughter Sarah was living. It was directly in the line of Egypt's march on Israel. She phoned Shlomo, a scholarly man who didn't look like the fighter he was in spite of his army uniform and the Uzi machine gun always on his rickety desk.

"Hello, this is *Kibbutz Revivim*. Oh, Golda! What's the situation? Can you tell us anything?"

Golda was tense and excitable these days, as was everybody else. "Shlomo, what can I tell you? Everybody who isn't mobilized is digging trenches in the parks. I never saw such tension in my life. May I speak to my daughter?"

"Sarah is out in the desert," Shlomo informed her. "Filling sandbags."

"But she's all right? She's feeling well?"

"She's fine. I'd put your son-in-law on but he's

out in the fields digging trenches."

"What about the children? Have they had enough drills? Do they know how to run to the shelters?" It was Grandmother talking, concerned, anxious about the little ones. Shlomo restrained a laugh.

"They know. They're well trained. Listen, Golda. Is the government considering that the best thing to do might be to sit tight and wait?"

"Wait for what?" she echoed bitterly. "For Russia to send the Arabs more tanks? Yesterday the Arab radio said, quote, 'The aim is to wipe Israel off the map.' Today they told Dayan they're going to put out his other eye. Should we wait for them to come and do it?"

"Golda—" Shlomo stammered, abashed.

"Get some sense, Shlomo. We must fight."

On the following morning, a Monday, the Six-Day War began—the one that was to electrify the universe and make them see for the first time that the Israelis were a fighting machine beyond belief. The Chosen of the Lord no longer turned the other cheek. They came pounding, churning, flying, shooting, and Nasser and Egypt stood shamed and dismal before the world. It was Israel's finest six days, something for history and the record books.

In the first three hours of the war Israeli aircraft knocked the Egyptian Air Force out of the skies and battered them on the ground, almost totally obliterating the finest of Russian equipment and fighter pilots. In the first three days Israel took the Gaza Strip and the entire Sinai. It was the 1956 Campaign repeated all over again—but with differences, of course.

On this momentous occasion Israeli soldiers took the concrete bunkers of the Syrians on the Golan Heights. And this time King Hussein of Jordan joined the Arab attack, and Israel took all of the Jordanian-held Palestine territory, including the Old City section of Jerusalem. It was a great, emotion-filled triumph for all Jews everywhere. After nineteen forlorn years, Jews were now able to visit their holiest of holies, the site of the Western Wall, where Jews had prayed and worshipped for centuries. Golda Meir was immensely satisfied, and happy to pay an official visit to the sacred place. With armed soldiers protecting the wall, Golda placed a reverent hand on the holy stones and began to weep. She was crying for all those who should have been able to share this great day with the victors but had not lived to see it.

When she became aware of someone nearby, she turned to see a young soldier, tired, his Sten gun on his shoulder, his forehead pressed against the stone wall—someone who was feeling exactly what she was feeling. He wanted someone to cry with, and then he saw Golda Meir. Recognizing her, he came to her wordlessly, placing his arms about her in a fervent embrace. She hugged him in silent accord, and they cried together, their tears blending. The armed sentries watched, their eyes filling. Golda's mind and heart were full of the moment.

Israel had defensible borders again. Was there anyone in the wide world who would dare to tell Israel to give them up again without a real guarantee of peace? Could they tell us to go home and start preparing our nine- and ten-year-olds for the next war? No! Not this time, world!

Tel Aviv, 1969.

A bus pulled over to its corner stop and Label Lazar, the driver, spotted the famous old woman standing there waiting for him, an armful of groceries loading her down. The stoic face, the boxy dress, the matching handbag—Mrs. Golda Meir! *The* Golda Meir.

"*Shalom*, Golda! My name is Label Lazar. I'm new on this route. Welcome to my bus." And he took the bag of groceries from her tired arms.

"What are you doing?" she protested.

"Golda Meir shouldn't have to carry groceries."

"Golda Meir can carry groceries like everybody else. I'm a private citizen again, thank God."

"I'm sure He doesn't know it yet," Label Lazar said briskly. "Wait till He finds out."

He gestured her sweepingly into his bus.

He knew Royalty when he saw it. Golda clambered aboard, grateful for his help. Now everyone on the bus was waving, calling out their greetings. She smiled. Label Lazar placed her grocery bag on the seat behind his, so Golda Meir sat there. The bus began moving. Golda fished in her handbag for coins for the metal box of fares.

Lazar called over his shoulder, "You still live in that little house on Baron Hirsh Street?"

She confirmed that. "Now I have time to enjoy it."

"I'm taking you to your door."

"Oh, no, Mr. Lazar, please! You're not allowed!"

Label Lazar chuckled. The other passengers exchanged appreciative glances.

"I am capable of walking home from the bus stop," Golda said, with the asperity of the old.

"You're too tired from shopping," he disagreed breezily.

"I am not tired."

"Well, *I'm* tired From the thought of letting you walk."

"If *you're* tired," Golda Meir snapped haughtily, "then drive yourself home."

Her fellow passengers roared with laughter. The bus echoed with their mirth. Label Lazar would not give up; turning, he sang out to the passengers, "Okay! Will the Cabinet give me a vote of confidence to drive Golda home?"

Everyone was cheering and applauding him now. Lazar was demonstrating the feistiness and toughness that made Israel what it was. In the end, he and the passengers overcame her objections and won. The bus rolled to a slow stop before her home. When she alighted with her bag of groceries, she was smiling and the passengers and Label Lazar were bidding her farewell with deep affection. The bus rolled away and she turned to her front door. Then the smile faded. Trouble again.

A semicircle of parked cars crowded the area

before the house on Baron Hirsh Street. Reporters and photographers surged forward when they saw her. Strobe lights began to flash. Again, as always, she knew something serious had happened. Israel and its world were not interested in gossip and scandal items, as some other countries were.

"What is it?" she exclaimed. "What happened?"

"Mrs. Meir." A reporter she knew, named Echod, spoke up first. "We know how you must feel. But some of us were at the *Knesset* and everybody's saying there's only one solution— Golda must come back!"

She shook her head, confused. The reporters were all so noisy. "What are you talking about?"

"You don't know?" Another friend, reporter Shtey, looked surprised.

"Know what?"

"Levi Eshkol," Shtey said quietly. "He had a heart attack and died."

"Oh, my dear God . . . Eshkol." The sad world closed in on her again. For a moment she swayed, then caught herself. Echod shot the next query at her. "Would you be willing to take over as Prime Minister?"

"Please, I don't even understand what you're saying. Please, please, leave me alone." She started for the door of her house. The reporters followed her like a tide that would not be denied. They let her find her way to the door in peace, yet they had spoken for everyone—for all Israel, it seemed. Everybody Jewish seemed to feel that

Golda Meir was the only one who could unite the country in its hour of trouble and need. Mrs. Lou Kaddar shared that opinion with the others.

In the King David Hotel that night, where they met for dinner and to talk the matter over, Lou Kaddar was very insistent on the subject of Golda Meir's becoming Prime Minister. Golda heard all her arguments with tolerant friendship. Lou could be very persuasive. But Golda was worried, just the same. She hardly touched her tea.

"Eshkol told me I was the only one who could unite the party. Now it's the whole country!" She shook her head sadly. "I came here to live in a *kibbutz* and help build a homeland in a plain, simple way. I don't want to be Prime Minister!"

"Golda," Lou Kaddar said pointedly, not sparing her old friend, "If you don't take the job, the leading contenders will practically fight a civil war over it."

"That we don't need," Golda agreed drily. "It's enough the Arabs insist they're still at war with us. But who knows if I could get elected? I'm a seventy-year-old grandmother, Lou."

"But you're in good health, right?" Lou Kaddar had never lost her suspicions and fears on that subject.

"Well—" Golda stalled, not wanting to really lie. "Being seventy is no joke. But it's not a sin, either." Suddenly she sighed. "Oh, Lou. I was really enjoying my retirement."

"Like hell you were," Lou Kaddar said with

acid truth.

The *Knesset*, with parliamentary finesse, elected Mrs. Golda Meir to the high post of Prime Minister of Israel by a vote of seventy to nothing. The unanimous tally made Golda bury her face in her hands and weep copiously. All about her, everyone was standing up, applauding, cheering the verdict. The hall rang with her triumph. And then she had to rise to her feet and go to the podium to make her acceptance speech. Yelling subsided as she began speaking.

"Some of our friends in other countries have expressed concern that Israel, by maintaining strong armed forces, may become militaristic. I can only answer that I am not in favor of a nice, liberal, antimilitaristic and dead Jewish people. . . ."

There was more applause and thunderous approval of those words.

"But on the other hand, the victories that we have won have never intoxicated us. They have never made us forget out great hope, our great desire, which is for peace. A peace that means good neighborly relations with the Arab people is fundamental to the Jewish renaissance. With all my heart I pledge that this government will make every effort in its power to bring about a true and everlasting peace."

She stepped off the podium and waves of love, admiration and acclaim engulfed her where she stood. Lou Kaddar wept with joy.

The Jewish National Anthem is *Hatikvoh;*

some spell it *Hatikva*. But however it is spelled, it means the same thing, the one thing Israel and the Jews had needed since the beginning—hope. They had clung to it for two thousand years.

Washington, D.C., 1969. The White House.

President Richard Milhaus Nixon greeted Prime Minister Golda Meir of Israel, in a red carpet reception with the Marine Band playing on the wide green lawn. Seldom had the band played better or more appropriately. The corps musicians did themselves and America proud with a spirited rendition of *Hatikvoh*.

Prime Minister Meir's day was a triumph, watched joyfully by all Israelites on television. The rest of the world watched, too, as Golda used the occasion to present what she called her "shopping list" to President Nixon and his Secretary of State, Henry Kissinger. The list requested the arms needed for the defense of Israel.

Bus driver Label Lazar, at home with his wife and children, kept his eyes glued to the TV. Pride overwhelmed him. "How do you like my Golda, hmmmm?"

Mrs. Lazar turned to the children goodhumoredly. "*His* Golda. I think your father's falling in love."

Label Lazar laughed. "I would, but what a line I would have to stand on!"

He spoke the truth. All Israel loved Mrs. Golda Meir. She was *Golda* to the Gentiles too—most of whom also loved her.

The Prime Minister of Israel's house became the very center of the political scene. In Jerusalem a typical day for Golda Meir would begin in the office, but inevitably it would continue in her home. Often she would meet with one group of cabinet ministers in her kitchen and there, discussing international problems with the coffee-pot in her hand, she would resolve the affair. At the same time, with other ministers in her living room, some domestic problem would be looked into and straightened out.

She was supposed to go to bed by midnight, at least—a woman of her advanced years. But it didn't always work out that way. And she smoked endlessly, one cigarette after another. It went on like this, nonstop, for a long time, until the fateful night when, sitting at her desk writing, her face suddenly contorted with pain and a great fear overcame her. Groping for the phone, breathing raspingly, she managed to dial Lou Kaddar's number.

"Lou . . . come and get me. . . ."

Lou Kaddar came, took one look at Golda Meir, and then bundled her downstairs into the official car and ordered the driver to speed to their destination. There were two security men with them. Hadassah Hospital was the next stop. Horrified at sight of Golda's pain-wracked face, Lou was taking her to Dr. Landau. She had never known Golda to look so awful and so weak.

"Slow down, Shimon," Golda called to the driver. "I don't want to be stopped . . . not now. Lou, were you able to reach Dr. Landau?"

233

"He'll meet you at the staff entrance in the rear, Golda."

"Did you order white coats?"

"Yes, I ordered the coats." Lou Kaddar was disapproving and suspicious. "But what's the point of all this secrecy? Suppose it does come out that your leg still bothers you from the shrapnel of that grenade in the *Knesset*—what of it?"

Prime Minister Meir smiled. "Politicians have a way of blowing things all out of proportion—especially opposition-party politicians."

Lou Kaddar subsided. There was just no arguing with Golda. She had an answer for everything.

The limousine sped through the darkness, carrying a very sick old woman.

Lights were burning in the Hadassah Hospital when they got there, but no one was in sight. Two cars pulled up—the one bearing Golda, Lou and the security men, and a backup vehicle containing more protective guards. Golda was led from her machine by the two agents with her; Lou Kaddar followed. They all went into the building.

In the anteroom entrance to the main offices, Dr. Landau was waiting for them. Golda and five security men were handed the white coats and Golda was assisted into hers by Avi. It was the Avi of the Zoe Village happening, long ago; he had been with Golda Meir ever since. Golda chuckled at Avi's frown as he viewed the white coat in his hands.

234

"Put it on," she commanded. "Everybody puts the coats on."

"May I ask why?" Avi wanted to know.

"So you'll all look like doctors. In a hospital, five doctors attract less attention than five ex-paratroopers. Either put it on or stay here," she concluded crisply.

Avi turned to his men. "Put the coats on."

He slipped into his own and Golda adjusted it on him personally, buttoning one button after another. She smiled warmly. "My, you look very nice, Avi. Your mother always wanted you to be a doctor, didn't she?"

Everybody laughed.

Golda Meir did not see Lou Kaddar slipping quietly into the anteroom behind her. Lou Kaddar had to know the truth for her own peace of mind. She was aware that something was radically wrong. It had to be, for all this to be going on so furtively—no matter what Golda had told her. Mrs. Lou Kaddar was not born yesterday.

The security men and Golda marched through the subterranean hallways. In their white coats they all looked very official. Finally Dr. Landau drew her out of earshot of the others, but Lou Kaddar was not very far behind. Landau reassured Golda Meir.

"What we have to do now is simply begin the therapy that we've already discussed. Treatments twice a week. I've arranged them for after midnight."

"And if there are leaks?"

"We're treating you for shrapnel in your legs."

Dr. Landau smiled conspiratorially.

Golda Meir nodded, satisfied. "Remember," she reminded him once more. "If it makes my hair fall out . . . just one little hair. . . ."

They had come to a white door. Dr. Landau opened it. The word on the door, painted boldly in black, was RADIOLOGY. Golda looked at the meaningful word, then suddenly turned, sensing Lou Kaddar's presence somewhere behind her. For a moment the eyes of the two old friends held. Golda's slow nod might have been the words, "So now you know." Lou Kaddar tried to smile bravely. She couldn't.

She could do nothing but hand Golda Meir a cigarette, and light it for her. Golda put her hand on Lou's as if to steady the lighting-up process. She blew a puff of smoke and then extinguished the light with a breath. She held on to Lou Kaddar's hand for a moment longer; then she turned to the open door and went inside. Dr. Landau had already preceded her into the room. There were tears in Lou Kaddar's eyes. No one had to ask why.

The limousine with the American flag flying gaily from its hood drew up to Prime Minister Golda Meir's house in bright Jerusalem sunlight. Security men, stationed out of doors, moved quickly to meet it. Senator John Durward was coming to talk to Mrs. Golda Meir. As Simcha Dinitz, one of her cabinet, had told her: "This is a very important man. He holds the key vote on the Senate Armed Services Committee."

"Friendly or unfriendly, Simcha?"

"Said to be a friendly type personally. On Israel, however, not sympathetic. Never has been."

Dinitz was the one to usher Senator Durward into the Prime Minister's presence. "Good afternoon, Senator. I'm Simcha Dinitz, Mrs. Meir's political secretary. Won't you come in, please?"

In Golda's living room they all stood stiffly while introductions were made. Protocol prescribed that they all stand. Golda and the senator were giving each other the once over, not so lightly. There was political tension in the air.

"Madame Prime Minister, how do you do?"

"I'm very happy to meet you, Senator. Won't you sit down? Would you care for coffee?"

"Very kind of you."

"And a little something to go with it? Are you hungry?"

"No, no. Just coffee's fine."

Golda went into her kitchen and disappeared. But when she put the percolator on a gleam came into her eye. Soon she was at the refrigerator, pulling things out. In the living room, Senator Durward frowned impatiently, looking at his watch. She had been gone for more than five minutes.

He growled at Dinitz, "What's she doing in there?"

Simcha Dinitz smiled. "Making coffee."

"You mean herself?"

"And if I know her, a little something to go with it."

Durward shook his head incredulously. He looked at his watch once more. The time interval had lengthened. A man of action, he strode to the kitchen door, opened it partway, and called, "Excuse me!"

Golda Meir was exercising her culinary skills as Durward put his head into her kitchen.

"Ah, Senator. Just in time. I hope you like honey cake—this is my own recipe. Sit down."

Dumbfounded, he watched her set things on the kitchen table. Suddenly he could only smile at the sight of this remarkable old woman of whom he had heard so much, pottering around the kitchen like a hausfrau. Senator John Durward did as he was told—he sat down.

"Terrific," he said, making himself comfortable, smelling the appetizing cake set before him. "Matter of fact I had to skip lunch today. The schedule was hectic."

"You see? Nobody's ever hungry, but what I serve they don't refuse."

The senator took a bite. "Mmmm. Delicious."

"I'll just take this out to the boys and be right back."

She carried a tray full of food through the kitchen door and bustled out. Senator Durward tried a bite of matzoh ball and liked it very much. Then he suddenly did a double take, staring after the Prime Minister of Israel in complete disbelief. What kind of woman was this? He was soon to find out, to his great joy.

On her patio, while the senator waited in her

kitchen, Golda set out her dishes on the table for the security men and Avi. "And if you don't care for the menu, it's your own fault. I told you to go home."

"Golda," Avi complained. "You know we have to be relieved."

"I don't need anybody today. I won't be going out any more."

"Golda, we have our orders."

"But I won't tell, I promise!"

Avi could only look at the other security men and groan. "*Oy, veh*," quoth Avi.

Senator John Durward and Prime Minister Golda Meir became great friends that day. They spoke each other's language. "I don't remember when anything hit the spot like this."

"I'm glad you enjoyed it."

"Can I help you with the dishes?"

"You can help me, Senator. But not with the dishes."

When she took off her apron Senator Durward could see the instant transformation. Gone was the hausfrau; this was now the woman who was Prime Minister of Israel, Mrs. Golda Meir.

In Golda's study they talked long into the night.

Durward was thoughtful. "Well, in addition to the Starfighter, I could try for Congressional approval to sell you M-551 tanks."

"But the Starfighter is not the plane we need."

"What's wrong with it?"

"The Egyptians are flying Russian MIG Twenty-Ones, with a speed of thirteen-eighty mph, comparable to the Starfighter's, and a range of 680 miles, better than twice the Starfighter's. Also the Starfighter is an unstable airplane with an unacceptable record of crashes. We can't afford to lose pilots in combat, let alone in accidents. The plane we need is the Phantom."

"Let's talk tanks."

"The Egyptians have the Russian T-62, an excellent tank. It's faster than your M-551 Sheridan. And it has heavier armor."

"But the Sheridan carries a heavier cannon."

"Yes, but. The Sheridan is too light for the recoil of such a heavy cannon; it shakes the laser rangefinder out of alignment. Also the Sheridan has a blind spot at a range of one thousand to twelve hundred yards. Senator, please sell us the M-Sixty."

Senator Durward came up for air and looked at Prime Minister Meir in genuine amazement.

"My dear lady, how can you be up on all this?"

She smiled, a bitter smile, and looked at him gently.

"Oh, Senator, don't you think I'd rather be up on schools, housing, farming, industry? We have no choice. After the Six-Day War, we pleaded with the Arabs to negotiate peace, and they came back with their famous three no's: no negotiation, no recognition of Israel, no peace. The position of the PLO is that Israel must be destroyed, even within the prewar boundaries."

Durward wagged his head. "Oh, I'm sure the

United States would never let that happen."

"You remind me of your wonderful President Kennedy, may he rest in peace. He said to me, 'Mrs. Meir, nothing will happen to Israel. We are committed to you.' And I said, 'Mr. President, I believe you one hundred percent. I just want to make sure that by the time you honor your commitment, we're still here.'"

The senator looked at Golda Meir. He could not hold back an appreciative grin. *This was a woman.* It was too bad that John F. Kennedy was not alive to see her now, in all her latter-day glory. What stories he would have to tell of her when he went back to the States, with her suggestions and proposals and offers. All in all, she was a very shrewd, brilliant woman, a true leader, as far as Senator John Durward was concerned.

The war room of the Israeli Army, commonly known as "the pit," was filled with the *crême* of Israel's defense people—Golda Meir, Moshe Dayan, Galili and other top cabinet members. General David Elazar, chief of staff, was using his long pointer on the war map, trying to make the picture clear to all those present.

"The Egyptian buildup is along the full length of the Suez Canal. It amounts to one hundred thousand men and over two thousand tanks." His words, doom filled, echoed hollowly in the subterranean war room. High-ranking officers nodded in agreement for the benefit of Israel's high command people. The outlook was grim enough without lying.

Elazar went on, "Without calling up the reserves, eighty-five hundred men and two hundred seventy-six tanks." He moved the pointer along the expanse of colored map. "The Syrians have forty-five thousand men against our five thousand, seventeen hundred tanks as compared with our one hundred seventy-seven." He paused, waiting for comment.

Golda Meir stirred. "What does Intelligence say?"

A colonel named Talmi answered that question. "We don't see the Syrians attacking us. We think they somehow got the idea we may attack them."

"And the Egyptian buildup, Colonel?"

"If Nasser were still alive we'd be concerned. But Anwar Sadat is a cooler head. Sadat simply has his army on maneuvers."

"So—" Golda Meir looked around the room. "Nobody thinks we should call up our reserves?"

Nobody answered her. In fact, they all seemed sheepish.

"Is this because nobody wants to upset the country, three days before *Yom Kippur*?" Observance of the Jewish High Holy Day, one of the two that has the greatest hold on the Jewish heart, mind and conscience, could be the reason for such procrastination. General Elazar disagreed.

"It's not a matter of *Yom Kippur*, Golda. Our best intelligence, including input from the Americans, is that there will be no war." A murmur filled the room, agreeing with him.

That was the end of the discussion that day. Everyone went home or back to their desks to wonder and think some more, and to consider what the consequences would be if they were wrong. For Golda Meir, it was but one more hour of trial and ordeal. Prime ministers are the first to be blamed when their generals are wrong.

As events turned out, the generals were dead wrong, and Israel faced disaster once more.

Egypt was prepared to annihilate Israel again, this time for keeps.

## *Mrs. Meyerson*

---

On the patio the next day, at Golda's house, she
had some coffee with Lou Kaddar. She was still
very much troubled by the discussion in the war
room. Something told her things were not quite
right. Her Jewish nose for trouble in the wind was
working overtime.

"My instincts tell me to mobilize, Lou. But the
facts are that it would cost millions and just
about cripple industry, business and essential
services. So how can I go by instinct?"

"Especially when the best military minds in the
country are against it," Lou Kaddar reminded her
drily.

"Oh, it wasn't only the general staff. We had a
cabinet meeting and the vote was unanimously
against mobilization."

"So there you are, Golda."

Avi the security man loomed into view, holding
an envelope. "Excuse me; this just came." Golda
took the envelope, smiling. "Thank you. Go home
to your family, Avi. It'll be *Yom Kippur* soon."

Avi looked at Lou Kaddar and just shook his head, then walked away. Golda digested the message that had been sent, reading it aloud for Lou Kaddar's benefit. It was but one more intelligence report.

"Soviet transport planes are in Syria, evacuating the families of Russian military advisers. This does not alter our current assessment of the situation."

Golda Meir crumpled the note in alarm. Lou Kaddar shook her head, as Avi had. Was Intelligence mad? This certainly did not sound too good. Golda lifted her coffee cup and sipped slowly. When she set it down, she said, softly: "Idiots. Are they all idiots in Intelligence?"

Lou Kaddar had no answer for that remark.

On the eve of *Yom Kippur*, that most sacred of Jewish holidays, many Jews traditionally have a family dinner before the fast begins. This year, Golda Meir just could not sit at the table. She left early and went to bed, bone weary, mind weary. But the red telephone in her bedroom showed her no mercy that night. It rang urgently, at several minutes past four in the morning. Waking quickly, Golda answered the phone with fear in her heart. It was Serious Time again; it had to be, at such an hour. It was. Golda knew that as soon as she heard Colonel Talmi's voice. It had worry in every syllable.

"This is Talmi. We have reliable information that Syria and Egypt will both attack this afternoon."

246

"Have you informed Dayan and Dado?"

"Yes. They've made a staff decision to call up reserve units for the defense line immediately. They say they need your approval for the next phase—and how soon can we meet in your office?"

"How soon?"

Golda Meir was not well. She shut her eyes, trying to think. For the moment her first thought was that she would never forgive herself; she should have overruled her cabinet and everybody else and ordered mobilization. Was it only yesterday that the fate of Israel had been in her hands? No, she would never forgive herself. But it was a little late for that.

Into the red phone she murmured: "I'm on my way, Talmi."

The pain in her, the sickness, continued to build as she began to dress to fly to her office.

Dr. Landau's diagnosis of her building illness had been all too accurate. Treatments or not, the pain was a steady thing lately. She was a sick woman, Prime Minister or not, war or not.

Moshe Dayan, General Elazar, Galili and Colonel Talmi were all there waiting for her in the office. Daylight had begun to ebb in from the outside. The new day was dawning. Israel's last day? She did not know. The worried faces of her colleagues were far from cheering. And Golda Meir's head was a dull center of constant aching.

Elazar minced no words. "The first decision concerns calling up additional units at this time."

"Call them up," Prime Minister Meir said.

"On the next point, the defense minister and I are not in agreement, Golda. Our air force can strike at noon if you give me the green light."

Dayan rose against that, scowling angrily. "That would be a pre-emptive strike. I'm against it because it would get us labeled the aggressors."

Elazar and Dayan both looked to Golda for the answer. She looked at Galili, dismayed. Talmi could be no help here.

"Two brilliant generals," she mocked, "and I have to decide?"

"Yes," Galili said. "Because this is not strictly a military issue. This is political." He was adamant.

Golda sighed. "Dado, I know that your approach can save lives up front. But we don't know what's in the future. Suppose it turns out that we need help? If we strike first, we'll get nothing from anyone." She took a breath. "No pre-emptive strike. That's it."

General David Elazar—Dado—shrugged. Moshe Dayan smiled.

As it turned out, Golda Meir and Moshe Dayan were both wrong. Indeed, they were to be criticized for the rest of their lives for their part in what came to be known as the Yom Kippur War. Some would call them hawks, others doves, and no one would know the actual truth. Only one unalterable reality remains until this very day. At two p.m. on *Yom Kippur*, October 6, 1973, the Syrians shelled Israeli positions, and then attacked.

* * *

In the south the Egyptians crossed the Suez Canal along its entire length, with legions of soldiers and hordes of tanks, crossing on pontoon bridges. Egyptian soldiers raised their flag on the east bank of the canal. The Arab tanks came rolling and firing too. The Arab soldiers cheered as they crossed. Israel was doomed.

The first three days of fighting threatened disaster for Israel. The Egyptian Army overran Israel's strongpoints on the renowned Bar-Lev line. Their armored columns raced toward the critical desert passes. In the north the situation was even worse. The Syrian Army broke through the Golan Heights, heading for the dozens of farm settlements below. Meanwhile the Israeli mobilization, off to a very late start, was taking too much valuable time. Days were needed to assemble soldiers and transport them; for the soldiers themselves it took time to adjust from running a desk or a harvesting machine or a lathe to facing the rigors of the battlefield.

On Jerusalem streets, Israeli tanks began to churn toward the front with young men and old manning them. The sight of their Prime Minister, Golda Meir, running along with them, waving, was inspirational. "*Golda! Golda!*" they called.

Reaching out to touch the passing hands stretching down to her, Prime Minister Meir had to choke back the tears. Which of these fine men would be dead before the fighting ended? War was hard to bear and to understand. Being Prime Minister did not help; somehow it only made the war worse for Golda Meir.

* * *

In Washington, D.C., Ambassador Simcha Dinitz sleepily answered his phone. Dinitz was in his shirtsleeves and very tired. His new post had kept him busier than even he had ever imagined. His caller was the Prime Minister of Israel.

"Yes, Golda?"

She sounded brisk. "Well, has the airlift started?"

"Not yet, Golda."

"What do you mean not yet? You should have seen our kids going off to the front, not knowing they won't have any air cover!"

Dinitz didn't like being shouted at, even by her. "Golda, I'm aware that. . . ."

She cut him off in midsentence. "You can't imagine how frightening the situation is. We've already lost almost half our fighter planes, not in air battles but to missiles. Russian missiles fight against us on both fronts. And our tank losses are just as bad!"

He heard the misery in her voice then. It made him contrite. "The Defense Department doesn't want to send us arms in U.S. planes," he explained. "I'm shopping around for other carriers."

"It's too late for shopping! President Nixon promised to help us if we needed help—tell him we do, and it has to be today! Tomorrow we may be completely overrun. Call Kissinger and tell him! Call the senator who liked my cake! Call them right now, Simcha!"

Never had her voice sounded so urgent in his ear. Simcha Dinitz shook himself. "Golda, do you know what time it is here? I'm not sleeping, God knows, but they are."

Golda Meir barked very emphatically over the long-distance line, "Tell Kissinger he can sleep when the war is over!"

America kept its promise. President Nixon personally ordered C-5 Galaxies to deliver tanks, rockets and medical supplies to stricken Israel. The fighter planes, denied permission to land in any of the European democracies for purposes of refueling, had to do so in midair. And on the ninth day of the war the long overdue American airlift finally reached Israel. The Lydda Airport Ramp was a setting for joy unrestrained as the valuable supplies came rolling down the cargo chute.

Golda Meir thanked her personal God for rejecting the temptation to strike first. She was still sure in her mind that this life-saving airlift would not have been granted by the U.S. if Israel had struck first against Egypt and the Arabs. But what a price Israel had paid for that choice—her choice, and Moshe Dayan's. Some would call Golda Meir a hawk in politics and claim that this provoked the Yom Kippur War. Others would call her dove, citing her failure to pursue intelligence reports concerning the Arab military buildup preceding the conflict, leaving Israel unprepared and just not ready for the onslaught when it came. Dayan would have his detractors too, though no one would ever deny the personal courage and character of both of them.

Israeli trucks and planes and troops fought

251

back, deploying their war machines along the Sinai, streaking across the blue skies, strafing, burning out the Russian tanks as they roared across the land. The fighting was fierce, intense, without letup. Gains were being made, but Israel's future life was still very much in the balance. The fortunes of war had not been decided yet.

General David Elazar phoned Golda Meir from the heat of the battle, using a field telephone from the desert. "I'm at the canal with Shayke's division, Golda."

The mother in her surfaced as always. "Don't be such a hero. You're the Chief of Staff; you're supposed to be in the map room!"

"Dayan and I are just looking things over. Listen, Golda . . . can you hear me?"

"Yes, Dado. I hear." Her heart was in her throat.

She could not see his wide grin. "We are back to being ourselves. And they are back to being themselves. And Golda . . . it will be all right."

"Oh, Dado. . . ."

"Yes, Golda. Yes."

"Thank God," she whispered fervently. Dimly she could hear field guns exploding over the line. She prayed to herself and hung up slowly.

Golda Meir, in her role of Prime Minister, made her verbal report to the *Knesset* on the following day. The parliament was so quiet a pin could have been heard dropping.

"On this, the tenth day of the war, I can tell you that we have a task force across the canal, operating in Egyptian territory." The applause came down from the rafters like a giant rolling wave. She waited for silence. "I want to thank God, and express our deep gratitude to the President and the people of the United States."

There was no measuring the tumultuous ovation these words elicited from all those present in the chamber. And this time there was no would-be assassin in the packed gallery to spoil things. It was a day of great happiness and hope in all Israel.

The Egyptian Army was learning all over again about Israel and how it could fight, when its back was to the wall. The never-say-die country and its people still lived.

By the sixteenth day, Israel had retaken virtually all of the Sinai and held a large area across the canal. The Egyptian Third Army was now completely encircled. In the north, Israel had regained all of the Golan and moved into Syria, within twenty-five miles of Damascus. At this point the harrassed Soviet Union began pressing for a cease fire. Generals began to ready themselves for meetings, to sign agreements of settlement. Crowds of Israelis began to collect at the Wailing Wall to pray and offer thanks. But there were still too many funerals in the land, and much grief, because of this Yom Kippur War. Victory had come at a great price. Prime Minister Golda Meir and her Defense Minister, Moshe

Dayan, came in for heavy criticism and abuse for the parts they had played in this war. Israel could not forget its most recent dead. They would not let Golda Meir and Moshe Dayan forget, either.

The mood in Israel was bleak and bitter. Battle casualties were the highest since the 1948 War of Independence. A kind of national trauma set in. Death was everywhere.

Golda Meir's ministry office became a constant setting for outraged mothers, waving their dead sons' dogtags in her very face. The weeping and wailing was like a thing alive, and Golda had to bear with it—as Dayan did, too. He faced the music with her.

"My son," one mother said, "when you called him up he ran off in such a hurry, he forgot his dogtags. So if he's dead, how will I ever know?"

Another mother at her side was not to be denied, either. "My son took his tags, so why don't I know? If he's dead, where's his body? If he's not dead he's a prisoner. Why can't anybody tell me that?"

Golda stood facing them, these crying, snarling women. She had to force herself to be calm, but it was not easy.

"We'll be getting a prisoner-of-war list from the Egyptians very soon. That's the agreement. From the Syrians, I don't know. They won't agree even to that."

Those were the mothers. Then the young men came with their complaints, just as angry and just as vocal. A young one named Amos hit her a very hard psychological blow indeed. "Every one of us was in the fighting and saw our friends die next to us. We have a right to ask—just when we had the enemy on the run, why did you agree to that cease fire?" The men with him all raised their voices in an assenting chorus of disapproval.

Prime Minister Meir steadied herself. "I wanted to hold out for real, negotiated peace this time. I've spent my life pleading for peace. But we are a very small country with a great and powerful friend. Sometimes we have to give in to that friend, even when we know we shouldn't."

The young warriors did not like that answer. They snapped at her, protesting she had betrayed them and all Israel.

And then a mixed group of men and women came to the office and let her know how they felt. It was no nicer, no better. "We blame *you* for the war," their spokesman, Abel, shouted at her. "Because Israel wasn't prepared! *You* should resign! And so should *he*!" He pointed an accusing finger at Moshe Dayan.

A woman named Deborah pushed forward past Abel. "Murderers!" she screamed.

Golda shook her head sadly. "Defense Minister Dayan offered to resign three times. I insisted that he stay."

Deborah was not appeased. Her face was contorted, her eyes bulged. "Murderers, both of you! Do you want to know what I tell my children? I tell them you killed their father!"

There was nothing one could say to that.

When the angry citizens had left, Golda and

Dayan looked at each other in a long, mutual silence. Their expressions were tragic. Golda was a weary lioness at her desk, a hand to her brow, the stoic face a grim comment on all that she had heard. Moshe Dayan, hurt by the accusations more than by any physical wound he had ever received, shook his head.

"Do they think we don't care? There's no way to fight a war without losses, especially when the other side attacks suddenly. The Americans had Pearl Harbor; the French, the Maginot Line; the British, Dunkirk. Those people seemed to understand."

"Our people are not like those people," Golda reminded him. "Do you supose, Dayan, that's why God chose us?"

Her gallows humor was lost on him this time. Moshe Dayan was too upset to laugh.

And yet the people of Israel elected Golda Meir for another four years as Prime Minister. She must have done something right as far as most of the country was concerned. And in her cabinet, at her personal insistence, was Moshe Dayan.

But only a few months after the election she found herself unable to continue. The dynamo was running down. Dr. Landau had the final word on that; in the end Nature had triumphed, as it always did. Golda was an old woman, a sick old woman.

"I told my key people I'm going to retire," she informed Landau in his office one day. "This time I better mean it. Isn't that right, Chaim?" There was almost a laugh in her weary voice.

"Yes," Dr. Landau said. His eyes showed his love for her.

"Well . . . I'm ready. I've done about everything I hoped to."

"And got yourself voted 'Woman Most Admired' in America. You couldn't have planned that, Golda."

"Woman Most Admired," she said slowly. "Would Morris vote for me? You know, if I had my life to live over, maybe there's one change I would have made. I think I would have stayed on the *kibbutz*."

"But what would the country have done without you?"

"Oh, believe me, Israel would have come through anyway. And I would have been more at peace with myself during my whole life."

Dr. Chaim Landau did not know about that. For himself, he could not imagine an Israel without a Golda Meir. The mere idea was an unhappy one. Israel had been blessed to have her!

"Why did you decide not to be Prime Minister anymore?"

Milwaukee again, 1977 once more. Another child asking one more question of the old woman on the platform. Golda Meir had talked long and warmly, filling in her past for them, and now yet there was another query. Golda smiled.

"There were a number of reasons. But one of them was that I was beginning to imagine people around me were whispering, 'For God's sake,

257

when is this old woman going to make up her mind that it's time for her to leave?' Maybe it wasn't all imagination."

A boy said, "You didn't want to be Prime Minister, anyway." Mr. Macy, the principal, smiled in approval. The children had been listening well.

"That's right," Golda responded. "I became one in the same way my milkman became commander of a machine-gun squad in the Seventy-three war. Believe me, he didn't want that job. But somebody had to do it."

Another boy raised his hand.

"You think there'll ever be peace between Israel and those other countries you mentioned?"

"Someday, yes." The old head bowed but the eyes twinkled with hope. "I believe—we must believe—that we'll have peace someday." She smiled out at the assemblage before her.

"When will that be?" the hand raiser persisted.

"When? I can tell you. When the Arabs love their children more than they hate us. That's when peace will come."

Golda Meir had said it all. Mr. Macy felt like cheering. So did the assistant principal. Mrs. Lou Kaddar smiled her eternal approval of Mrs. Golda Meir.

The golden visit, the magical tour of the past, with its triumphs, its defeats, its heartbreak and happiness, was over. Fourth Street School would never be the same again. Neither would the children.

* * *

Outside the school, Mrs. Golda Meir puffed on her badly needed cigarette, the limousine and the motorcade waiting on her pleasure. There had been a phone call and Mrs. Lou Kaddar had answered it as Golda waited. Golda was very tired. Talking to the children had been wonderful but the years had taken their toll again. She was worn out. The chauffeur assisted her into the car as Lou Kaddar came hurrying from the building. Mr. Macy and his staff waved farewell as the line of automobiles and motorcycles moved out once again. The day to remember was done. Golda settled back against her cushions.

"Well, Lou?"

"The call was from the embassy. Dinitz. They want you to cancel the rest of the trip and come home." The motorcade picked up speed.

"Who's 'they'?"

"Everybody," Lou Kaddar answered.

"What 'everybody'?"

"How about, your friends . . . and your enemies?"

Golda's stare was a trifle confused and Lou Kaddar launched into an immediate surprise.

"Golda, Sadat is coming to Jerusalem. Begin is going to meet him at the airport and take him to address the Knesset. Think of it!"

"Sadat is actually coming?" Golda Meir felt a stab of joy and wonder. "Not just talking about it?"

"Yes, yes."

"I'm not in the government," Golda said, slowly. "What do they need me for?"

Mrs. Lou Kaddar placed an arm on the arm of her old dear friend. Her eyes glowed. "Need you? You're part of history!"

"I'm ancient history, Lou. But if Sadat really wants to talk peace, I'd like to see somebody try and keep me away."

Of course, nobody did.

Anwar El-Sadat's plane came down out of the star-studded skies to land at Ben-Gurion Airport. When he emerged from the aircraft, a brown-faced, moustached man whose bald skull was framed by patches of black hair above the ears, there was an entourage of Jewish dignitaries to meet him, headed by Prime Minister Menachem Begin and Mrs. Golda Meir. Sadat's smile was a fixed thing, but when he came to Golda Meir he regarded her with something special in his gaze. His hand, when it took hers, squeezed warmly. It was another great moment for Golda Meir. The moon had seldom shone more brightly over Israel.

Later, in the Knesset, when Sadat made his speech, Egypt spoke and Israel and Golda Meir listened. Seldom had the Knesset been so packed. When Anwar El-Sadat had concluded his talk the place seemed to explode. It augured great things for Israel's future, and Golda Meir felt hope again in her heart.

After the Knesset there was a gathering in the Labor Party meeting room. A small army of cameramen from newspapers all over the globe had set up their equipment. Sadat,

260

stationed behind a bank of microphones, continued explaining his views. This was what everyone had come for, to hear what he had to say.

"There are differences, very serious differences," Sadat said, "but I agree that Israel must have security. And I am sure we have started the proper approach to the whole problem. Incidentally, an undeniable role in bringing about this effort for peace has been played by my former honest foe, your former Prime Minister, Golda Meir." Stepping back, he gestured for her to speak. There was heartfelt, energetic, applause. All eyes turned toward Mrs. Golda Meir. She smiled, happy, complete, fulfilled.

"This wonderful step that President Sadat has taken in coming here, proves that talking to each other through middle persons is not the same as meeting face to face. On our differences about the Palestinians, I believe there is a solution in a peace treaty with Jordan that will be good for them and safe for us. And now let me say something to President Sadat." She turned to him, to find him smiling at her.

"As an old lady—you always called me 'the old lady,' you know—" She could not go on for a moment, as everyone who heard was laughing. Sadat himself grinned widely, chuckling. Golda Meir regained control. "As an old lady, my great hope is that I'll live to see the day of peace between you and us. And as a grandmother to a grandfather—although you're just a new grandfather—I have a little gift for your granddaughter."

She handed Sadat a small gold box with a ribbon around it. There was more laughter, more applause. The President of Egypt accepted the gift and shook hands with Mrs. Golda Meir.

Later, many people would ask what the gift was. Lou Kaddar knew. It was a small gold locket, something a little girl would appreciate, someday.

The *Knesset* banquet hall, that night, was festive and beautiful. In am ambience of Chagall tapestries and Old World mosaics, the many guests at the individual tables could not take their eyes off the head table and the raised podium and lectern there. There was a master of ceremonies, of course, but the main attractions were Egypt's Anwar El-Sadat and Menachem Begin, Israel's own. At an individual table out front, Golda Meir sat with Mrs. Lou Kaddar.

"Ladies and gentlemen," the smiling M.C. began, when the small talk and clatter had died down, "the Honorable Achmed Mahandi, Deputy Foreign Minister of Egypt."

Mahandi mounted the podium to applause, a prepared speech in hand that looked fairly substantial. Lou Kaddar unhappily consulted her wrist watch. When Mehandi was at last done, the master of ceremonies intoned, "Ladies and gentlemen, I now have the honor to present to you the President of Israel, His Excellency Ephriam Katzir."

The applause came again and once more Lou looked at her watch. When Katzir spread the pages of his speech on the lectern, Lou Kaddar groaned. Golda shushed her and smiled. Lou checked her watch. Katzir spoke a long, long time.

"By the time they get to you, Golda," she murmured, "will you still remember what you wanted to say?"

"Did you ever know me when I didn't have something to say?"

The President of Israel left the podium, acknowledging the handclapping, and the master of ceremonies waited for quiet again. "And now it is my privilege to present a truly great lady of our time—or any other time. She has been called the mother of Israel and the earth mother of her people. But mostly she is just called Golda. Ladies and gentlemen, *Golda Meir!*"

Everyone in the banquet hall stood, including the dignitaries on the podium. All applauded vigorously.

As Golda Meir left her table and walked slowly across the floor to mount to the podium, stunning waves of affection and admiration came at her from all sides. She could feel it strongly, clear through to her old bones. She smiled, the stoic face unbending.

"Well," Gold Meir said quietly, as the applause settled down, "if I'm supposed to be the mother of Israel—earth mother, whatever kind of mother— I have a responsibility to be a good one. And what a good mother would say to you now is—" her pause was a thing of beauty—"it's late. Everybody go home." And she stepped down from the podium, just like that.

There was a moment of surprised silence; then the whole banquet hall erupted with a tremendous explosion of mirth, a roaring, quaking, building volcano of laughter. Everyone was on his feet again. The ovation was mammoth, unlike any ever heard in that hall before.

President Sadat himself was on his feet, laughing uproariously, applauding feverishly. Golda, passing his seat, leaned over and said, to be heard above the din, "Mr. President, I'll say good night."

"Good night, dear lady. I hope we see each other again."

"I'm glad you came," she replied softly, a touch sadly, somehow sensing that another meeting was not going to happen in this life.

"I am glad, too," Sadat said. "Very glad I came."

"So," Golda Meir said, her own woman to the end, "what took you so long?"

A lot of people have written and said a lot of things about Golda Meir at one time or other. For instance, "The miracle of Golda Meir was that she embodied the spirit of so many people—the hopes, the fears, the ideals and stubbornness of Jews everywhere."

"As a woman she was in the vanguard of all women striving for equality. As a person she was strong, she was warm. Unselfish. Totally honest." Somebody wrote that about her, too.

Well, as Mrs. Lou Kaddar said, Golda was all that—especially honest. God, was she honest. But as usual, Golda said it better than anybody else.

"Why am I known? Because of my wisdom, my great achievements? No. I am known because at a time of struggle for the Jewish people, I was one of a group that made it possible to have what we have, what we've been able to defend by the skin of our teeth. I did what I thought was right. And that's that. And after me, someone else will come, and I hope they'll do better."

*Shalom*, Golda, as Lou Kaddar said the day she died.

Golda Meir died in 1978 at the age of eighty. Like Moses, who led his people into the Promised Land but did not enter it, Golda did not live to see peace become a reality.

But she would have kept her sense of humor even if that point had come up. Everyone could be sure of that. She was the one who had once said, "Can you imagine Moses dragging us forty years through the desert to bring us to the one place in the Middle East where there is no oil?"

*Shalom*, Golda, indeed.

**PRICE:** $3.25  0-8439-1086-0  **CATEGORY:** Non-fiction
Hardcover

"I was carried away by this book, excited and eager to get back to it as to a good suspense novel."
—Book-of-the-Month-Club News

# INSIDE, LOOKING OUT

Harding Lemay

*INSIDE, LOOKING OUT* is the story of one man and the women who influenced his life. Spanning four decades, it ranges from the bleak farmlands near the Canadian border to the glamor of New York's theatrical and publishing milieus. It is a love story of a man who had the courage to stand apart, and the woman who had the courage to stand beside him.

The pulse-pounding sequel to ISLAND FLAME!

# SeaFire

Karen Robards

United by passion, they were torn from each other's arms by a nobleman's treachery!

# SEA FIRE

By
Karen
Robards

**PRICE:** $3.75
0-8439-1084-4

**CATEGORY:**
Historical
Romance

## Love and treachery on the high seas rekindle the passions of ISLAND FLAME'S tempestuous lovers, as their lusty, action-filled romance continues!

**L**ady Catherine had a genteel British upbringing and was living happily in America with her handsome husband and new son. Jon, her husband, had once been a murdering pirate with a quick temper and a fast sword. If anyone knew, he'd be hanging.

A POWERFUL SAGA OF HARDSHIP
AND FAITH ON THE GREAT TRAIL WEST

# WAGONS TO UTAH

## CLEE WOOD

LEISURE
1091
$2.25

# *WAGONS TO UTAH* Clee Woods

**F**orced to abandon their lifelong
homes in Illinois, the Wheelers forged
westward across the barren frontier with
few supplies, but complete faith in their
deliverance. They were led by the courage
and conviction of a man called Brigham
Young. The Wheelers were a devout
Mormon family. They shared a common
destiny, but each had their own desires.

**PRICE:** $2.25
0-8439-1091-7

**CATEGORY:**
Western

*Marguerite Tanner*

**M**arguerite had struck a bargain with life, trading her beauty, her only asset, for security. Now she had achieved the goals she had set for herself as a penniless young girl — wealth, position, a successful husband, attractive children. Then dynamic Lou Armitage entered her life. Consumed by a passion she could not control, Marguerite willingly risked the destruction of the very world she had so carefully constructed!

**By Elizabeth Dubus**

**PRICE:** $2.95
0-8439-1037-2
**CATEGORY:**
Novel

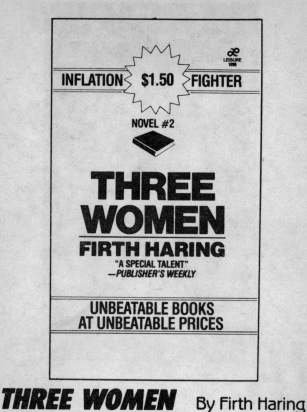

INFLATION $1.50 FIGHTER

æ
LEISURE
1096

NOVEL #2

# THREE WOMEN
## FIRTH HARING
"A SPECIAL TALENT"
—PUBLISHER'S WEEKLY

## UNBEATABLE BOOKS
## AT UNBEATABLE PRICES

# *THREE WOMEN*

**By Firth Haring**

PRICE: $1.50  0-8439-1096-8
CATEGORY: Inflation Fighter Novel

"A special talent"
—*Publisher's Weekly*

Ann was neurotic and bewildered in her
unhappy love affair with Freddy. Bootsie
was having an affair with her dead
husband's best friend. Louise was
enjoying her new life with Max—until she
found out what he had planned.
Three women, each in her own way,
desperately try to find love,
happiness—and themselves.

# THE REAPING

An ancient superstition reaches out, catching
you in a net of horror and suspense

# The Reaping

LEISURE
1035
$2.50

## BERNARD TAYLOR

"Taylor works wizardry again here."
—PUBLISHERS WEEKLY

**H**e was hired to paint the
portrait of a young woman at
Woolvercombe Mansion, but Tom
Rigby didn't know she was after
more than a painting. He wondered
about the identities of the strange
inhabitants of the house and the
bizarre events that began to
happen. And suddenly he was
catapulted into a rendezvous with
terror and violence, as the power of
the supernatural wielded its
horrifying spell!

## By Bernard Taylor

*CATEGORY:*
Occult
*PRICE:* $2.50
0-8439-1035-6

SEND TO: **LEISURE BOOKS**
**P.O. Box 511, Murray Hill Station**
**New York, N.Y. 10156-0511**

Please send the titles:

| Quantity | Book Number | Price |
|----------|-------------|-------|
| _____ | _____ | _____ |
| _____ | _____ | _____ |
| _____ | _____ | _____ |
| _____ | _____ | _____ |
| _____ | _____ | _____ |

In the event we are out of stock on any of your
selections, please list alternate titles below.

| | | |
|----------|-------------|-------|
| _____ | _____ | _____ |
| _____ | _____ | _____ |
| _____ | _____ | _____ |
| _____ | _____ | _____ |

Postage/Handling_____

I enclose_____

**FOR U.S. ORDERS, add 75¢ for the first book and 25¢ for
each additional book to cover cost of postage and handling.
Buy five or more copies and we will pay for shipping. Sorry,
no. C.O.D.'s.**

**FOR ORDERS SENT OUTSIDE THE U.S.A., add $1.00
for the first book and 50¢ for each additional book. PAY BY
foreign draft or money order drawn on a U.S. bank, payable
in U.S. ($) dollars.**

☐ Please send me a free catalog.

NAME _____

(Please print)

ADDRESS _____

CITY _____STATE _____ZIP_____

Allow Four Weeks for Delivery